THE GUINNESS SOCCER QUIZ BOOK

JULIAN FARINO

GUINNESS BOOKS

FOR TIG

Editor: Beatrice Frei
Design: David Roberts
Picture Editor: Alex Goldberg

© **Julian Farino and Guinness Publishing Ltd, 1989**

Published in Great Britain by Guinness Publishing Ltd,
33 London Road, Enfield, Middlesex

Photoset in Itek Bembo
by Ace Filmsetting Ltd, Frome, Somerset
Printed and bound in Great Britain by
Richard Clay Ltd, Bungay, Suffolk

British Library Cataloguing in Publication Data
The Guinness soccer quiz book
1. Soccer. Questions & answers
I. Farino, Julian
796'.076

ISBN 0-85112-368-6

Julian Farino is 27 and works as a researcher for Granada Television. After graduating from Cambridge in 1983 he was a sports editor for the *Guinness Book of Records* from 1984 to 1987. He has written two previous sports quiz books, *The Guinness Sports Challenge 1 and 2.* Julian follows the Crystal Palace football team.

The legendary Paslow FC. The author is standing second from the left.

ACKNOWLEDGEMENTS

Many thanks indeed to Rick and Steve Foster, both die-hard Crystal Palace supporters, for their great help.

I owe a debt to the Guinness collection of football books, especially those of the excellent writer and statistician Jack Rollin, on which I have leaned substantially. *The Book of Football Quotations* by Peter Ball & Phil Shaw (Stanley Paul) is well worth owning, too. Special thanks also to John English for editing and proofreading the text.

Pictures by All Sport and ASP

CONTENTS

CONTENTS

QUIZ 1

A - Z 1

The answer to each question begins with the letter indicated.

A   Centre forward for Oxford in the 1986 League Cup final

B   Leading scorer in Division One in 1982–3 season

C   Spain's captain in 1986 World Cup

D   Goalkeeper Andy, the officer of his defence

E   English club formerly known as St Domingo

F   Only Scottish club, apart from Falkirk, beginning with F

G   First club to play in all four divisions

H   Footballer of the Year in 1977

I   Nation that appeared in the World Cup finals for the first time in 1978

J   World Club champions in 1985

K   Rapid Vienna and Austria centre forward, Golden Boot winner 1978

L   They had an average home gate of 8038 in 1987–8 season

M   Scotland player who missed a penalty in 1978 World Cup match *v.* Peru whilst score was still 1–1 (Scotland lost 3–1)

N   They appear on the front cover of this book

O   Scored FA Cup final goal in 1978 but was immediately substituted

P   The dog that found the World Cup in 1966

Q   Blackburn and Northern Ireland striker

R   Luigi, Italian No 11 of the 1970s

S   At the start of 1989, Len Cantello was their assistant manager, Asa Hartford manager

T   Nation who held West Germany 0–0 in 1978 World Cup

U   Dozsa, European campaigners from Hungary

V   Home of Second Division club that sold Steve Bould to Arsenal

W   Over 50 caps for England, clubs included Manchester City and Werder Bremen

X   Current Paris St Germain player

Y   He took over Wales from England

Z   Surinamese midfielder who joined Ipswich from WBA

QUIZ 2

EUROPEAN & INTERNATIONAL 1

1   Who was the last Briton to be voted European Footballer of the Year?

2   Who is the most expensive German player ever?

3   Manchester United have never been knocked out before the semi-finals of the European Cup – true or false?

4   Who is the former Leeds player who has scored the most goals by a British player in European club competitions?

5   Which international star was transferred from Flamengo to Udinese for £2½ million in 1983?

6   Which Danish international has played a record total of 2273 mins of European Championship football?

7   In which continent is the Copa Libertadores contested?

8   Tom Finney won 76 caps for England; what was his main club side in that time?

9   Which Brazilian side were World Club champions in 1962 and 1963?

10   Who was the Argentinian full back who signed for Birmingham after Ardiles and Villa had led the way?

11   Which Spanish club side did John Toshack take over after leaving Sporting Lisbon?

12   For which nation does Gheorghe Hagi play?

13   What nationality is Joao Havelange, President of FIFA?

14 Which Brazilian star of the 1982 World Cup inspired Roma to their first Italian league title for 40 years?

15 Which country has famous club sides Penarol and Nacional?

16 How many Arsenal players were in the England team that played Italy in 1934?

17 In which country are PAOK Salonika one of the top sides?

18 Which was the first team from East Germany to win a European competition, the Cup Winners Cup in 1974?

19 Name the three Portuguese sides to have won European competitions.

20 In which country might Boca Juniors play Estudiantes?

QUIZ 3

MANAGERS 1

1 Who is the First Division's longest serving manager?

2 Who managed Everton to the club's seventh league title in 1970?

3 Who resigned as Scottish team manager in May 1977 to go to manage Hearts?

4 Which club did Alf Ramsey lead to Second and First Division championships in successive seasons?

5 Which former Manchester United player became the youngest manager in the league after his playing career ended prematurely?

6 Who was manager of Nottingham Forest immediately before Brian Clough?

7 Who managed West Germany to their 1974 World Cup triumph?

8 Which manager came out of retirement during the 1979–80 season to play one league game for Doncaster?

9 Lawrie McMenemy never played a Football League match. True or false?

10 Which player-manager was top scorer for Shrewsbury in the 1973–74 season?

11 Which of the following managers does not possess an OBE – Alex Ferguson, Bertie Mee or Brian Clough?

12 Who managed Lincoln City to the Fourth Division title in 1975–76?

13 . . . Which manager, who has since won the FA Cup, managed Hereford to the Third Division title in the same year?

14 Who managed Derby to their last championship title?

15 Which club did Dario Gradi lead to the top of the Fourth Division at the beginning of 1989?

16 Who led Aston Villa to the European Cup in 1982?

17 Who was the famous Arsenal goalscorer of the 1930s who went on to manage Chelsea's 1954–55 championship winning team?

18 Which other First Division manager was Best Man at George Graham's wedding?

19 Which manager is godfather to Terry Venables' daughter?

20 Name Jim Smith's two clubs before he joined Newcastle.

QUIZ 4

BRITISH FOOTBALL 1

1 Which club has played the most seasons in the First Division?

2 Who were the first Football League champions in 1888–89?

3 In which decade did a team last win the league on goal average or goal difference?

4 Rangers once shared the Scottish League title – with which club?

5 For how many games did Leeds remain unbeaten from the beginning of the 1973–74 season?

6 Who scored 410 league goals from just 408 games for Celtic, 1923–37, a record by a player for one league club?

7 Which team, currently in the Third Division, led the First Division at Christmas 1981?

8 . . . Who won the league that year, and where did Swansea finish?

9 In which year was the Football League re-organized and Divisions 3 and 4 started – 1946, 1951 or 1958?

10 Which club, in 1926, became the first to achieve a hat-trick of league championships?

11 Following the introduction of three points for a win, which (then) Fourth Division side became the first to register 100 points in a season?

12 The Scottish Football Writers first recognized a Player of the Year in 1965 – who was the Celtic man to be honoured?

13 Which was the first British club to 'go public' on the Stock Exchange, in 1983?

14 Which team won the Third Division in 1983–84 and the Second Division a year later?

15 Which team slipped from the First Division to the Fourth in successive seasons, 1979–82?

16 Ian Botham, Chris Balderstone and Brian Close all played in the Football League. True or false?

17 Who made most appearances for Leeds – Jackie Charlton, Billy Bremner or Johnny Giles?

18 Which was the first club to be promoted to the Fourth Division under the introduction of automatic promotion from the Vauxhall Conference?

19 Nottingham Forest won the league immediately after being promoted from the Second Division in 1976–77. True or false?

20 Which London side led the First Division at the beginning of October 1987?

PICTURE QUIZ 1

DOWN AND OUT OF SIGHT

Identify these four players.

1

2

3

4

QUIZ 5

QUOTES

1   Who said, in response to his new club's 10–1 defeat at Maine Road in November 1987, 'Three of their goals were offside'?

2   Which manager was David Lacey of *The Guardian* describing when he said his 'natural expression is that of a man who fears he might have left the gas on'?

3   'They used to say I was fat. Now they say I'm powerful.' Which Liverpool player said this?

4   'They are mad dogs and I am madder than the rest of them.' Which country's national manager described his team thus in Mexico in 1986?

5   'The nearest I come to football now is the weekly spot-the-ball competition.' Which former England manager said this?

6   Which former Liverpool and QPR midfielder, following his move to Spain, said 'I speak Spanish as badly as I speak English'?

7   'Barcelona may be the biggest club in the world, but they still owe me the train fare to London when they interviewed me for the manager's job.' Which manager, now in Spain, said this?

8   'I know nothing about the theft. I have never seen the bracelet.' Explain.

9   'If we lose we are boring, not entertaining. And when we win we are a load of thugs.' Which team is being described by their manager?

10   'Now it would take a really exceptional offer if I were to be tempted to leave Pittodrie.' Who said this, in October 1986?

11   Which Everton left-sided player was Howard Kendall describing when he said, 'It's so long since he scored that he'd forgotten how to leap and punch the air'?

12   'He doesn't give you the ball. He lends it to you for a second or two.' Which of his Manchester City players was Malcolm Allison describing?

13 About whom did George Best say in 1988, 'He's accused of being arrogant, unable to cope with the press, and a boozer. Sounds like he's got a chance to me'?

14 'It's Wales I want to go to, not Timbuctoo. I won't be away long enough for the tea to get cold.' Who said this?

15 Who, at the beginning of 1988, described Liverpool's 15 point lead as being helped by 'The poorest First Division I have seen'?

QUIZ 6

THE SIXTIES

1 Which club was elected to the league in 1962?

2 The first time a fee of £50 000 was paid by an English club was in March 1960. For whom did Manchester United pay Huddersfield?

3 Which member of England's World Cup winning side went on to become a funeral director?

4 Which team, currently in the Fourth Division, won the league in 1960?

5 How many times did Jimmy Greaves finish top or joint top scorer in Division One during the decade – 1, 3 or 5?

6 In which year was the maximum wage abolished – 1961, 1965 or 1969?

7 In 1969, Leeds won the league with a record 67 points. How many times were they beaten during the league season?

8 'Greaves dazzles in rout of Scotland' said the *Sunday Express* in 1961. What was the score of the international?

9 Which Scottish side reached the semi-finals of the Cup Winners Cup in 1968?

10 Who was the Brazilian goalkeeper who completed 100 caps in 1968?

11 'There's too much soccer already insist Tottenham' said

a national headline in 1960. To which new competition were they objecting?

12 In 1960, the first European Nations Cup (European Championships) was staged. Who were the winners?

13 Who was the player involved in the 1964 world record transfer of £440 000 between Varese and Juventus?

14 Who became President of FIFA in 1961?

15 In a World Cup qualifying game in 1964, riots caused the death of 300 people. Name either of the countries involved.

16 Bob Paisley is the most successful English manager in terms of trophies won with 13. Two others, prominent in the sixties, are next with eight – who are they?

17 Where was the 1962 World Cup staged?

18 Who retired in 1965 after scoring a record 434 league goals?

19 In 1964, Oxford created a record in the FA Cup for a Fourth Division club by reaching which round?

20 The Football League first allowed a substitute to be used in 1965 – what was the condition required for its use?

QUIZ 7

FA CUP 1

1 In which year did Fourth Division Colchester beat Leeds in the Fifth Round?

2 'Harry Gregg just after t'Final
Went into Nat's for a beer
Who returned his money and told him
We don't charge goalkeepers here'
To what incident in the 1958 final does this verse refer?

3 1927 marked the introduction of which song to the proceedings at Wembley?

4 Who scored Leeds' winning goal in the 1972 final?

5 Which club, in the period 1919–39, had the greatest success in terms of the average round reached?

6   Which amateur club held Manchester United to a draw at Old Trafford in 1953 despite odds of 75–1?

7   . . . And who was the man, a Test cricketer and commentator, who played on the wing for the underdogs?

8   Who, in 1982, missed an FA Cup final because of war?

9   Who was the losing team in the so-called 'Matthews Final' of 1953?

10   Which was the first club to appear in 10 FA Cup finals?

11   Who were the giant-killers of mighty Arsenal in 1933?

12   Which was the last Second Division side to win the Cup?

13   In the 1956 final, who was the Manchester City keeper who played the last 15 minutes with a broken neck?

14   Who became the youngest player to play in a final in 1966?

15   In 1973, Sunderland became the first Second Division side to win the Cup since the war. True or false?

16   . . . Who were the next to do so?

17   Who, in 1977, made his eighth appearance as player or manager in a final, but won for the first time?

18   Which player, in 1959, scored in the final for Forest, broke a leg, and watched on from a hospital TV set?

19   Who is the only player to score for two different clubs in FA Cup finals?

20   Which bottom of the table team beat top-place Liverpool in the Fifth Round in 1983?

QUIZ 8

MILESTONES

1   In which season was three points for a win first introduced?

2   Who, in 1979, became the first English club to adopt advertising on their shirts?

3   What was the score of the first Full Members Cup final between Chelsea and Manchester City?

4   In which decade was the first Football League match played under floodlights?

5   In which year did goal difference replace goal average – 1970, 1973 or 1976?

6   Which was the first British club to win a European competition?

7   Which Portsmouth player became, in 1964, the first man to reach 700 league appearances?

8   Who was the first Scottish player to win 100 caps?

9   In which year were two substitutes first allowed for FA Cup and Littlewoods Cup matches?

10   Which club was the first to achieve the League and FA Cup double?

11   In which year did Bobby Moore make his record 108th appearance for England?

12   In which decade was the law introduced to compel a keeper to stand still on the goal line for a penalty kick?

13   Which was the first British club to win the Fairs Cup?

14   In which season was the League Cup first contested?

15   In which decade were numbers first worn on shirts in an FA Cup final?

16   Which came first, the Freight Rover or the Sherpa Van?

17   In which year did Alf Common break the £1000 transfer barrier – 1905, 1925 or 1955?

18   Which player, later manager of Gillingham, was the league's first substitute?

19   In which World Cup final did a player first convert a penalty?

20   Which was the first British club to convert their stadium to an all-seater?

QUIZ 9

TRANSFERS 1-MILLION POUNDERS

In the three lists below, the players and their club moves have been jumbled up. You have to reassemble them.

PRICE	PLAYER	CLUB & DATE
£6 900 000	. . . Peter Beardsley	. . . . Everton – Barcelona, 1986
£5 500 000	. . . Steve Daley	. . . . . . Man Utd – AC Milan, 1984
£4 800 000	. . . Kevin Reeves	. . . . . Coventry – Notts Forest, 1980
£3 200 000	. . . Bryan Robson	. . . . . Newcastle – Liverpool, 1987
£2 750 000	. . . Andy Gray	. . . . Spurs – Rangers, 1987
£2 300 000	. . . Ruud Gullit	. . . . Wolves – Man City, 1979
£1 900 000	. . . Ian Wallace	. . . . Norwich – Man City, 1980
£1 500 000	. . . Clive Allen	. . . . Man Utd – Barcelona, 1986
£1 500 000	. . . Ian Rush	. . . . St Mirren – Rangers, 1988
£1 500 000	. . . Justin Fashanu	. . . . . Arsenal – Crystal Palace, 1980
£1 469 000	. . . Richard Gough	. . . . Notts Forest – Man Utd, 1980
£1 437 500	. . . Gary Lineker	. . . . . Birmingham – Notts Forest, 1979
£1 350 000	. . . Garry Birtles	. . . . . . PSV Eindhoven – AC Milan, 1987
£1 250 000	. . . Ian Ferguson	. . . . . . Aston Villa – Wolves, 1979
£1 250 000	. . . Diego Maradona	. . . Norwich – Notts Forest, 1981
£1 250 000	. . . Trevor Francis	. . . . Liverpool – Juventus, 1987
£1 250 000	. . . Ray Wilkins	. . . . . . Argentinos Juniors – Barcelona, 1982
£1 180 000	. . . Kenny Sansom	. . . . Palace – Arsenal, 1980
£1 000 000	. . . Diego Maradona	. . . Barcelona – Napoli, 1984
£1 000 000	. . . Mark Hughes	. . . . . WBA – Man Utd, 1981

QUIZ 10

WORLD CUP 1

Unless specified, all questions refer to World Cup final tournaments and not qualifying competitions.

1   Which is the only country to be ever-present at World Cup finals?

2   Which is the only country to have twice hosted the competition?

3   Which cricket star played for Antigua in the qualifying tournament of the 1978 World Cup?

4   Who managed Argentina to the trophy in 1978?

5   Which was the nation, competing for the first time, who took a shock lead against Italy in 1974 before losing 1–3?

6   Who became the first player to miss a penalty in a World Cup final in the 1982 Italy – West Germany match?

7   Who beat England 4–2 in the 1954 competition?

8   Which was the first country to retain the World Cup?

9   Who was the Brazilian who, in 1962, became the first player to score in two World Cup finals?

10 Which two countries were involved in the 1982 semi-final when penalties were used to decide the game for the first time?

11 In which year did England take part for the first time?

12 In which year did Brazil win the Jules Rimet trophy outright?

13 England beat Portugal in the semi-final in 1966. Who did West Germany beat in the other semi-final?

14 In which year did Scotland first compete?

15 When Wladyslaw Zmuda of Poland achieved his 20th appearance in finals matches, which West German's record did he equal?

16 Who scored Northern Ireland's goal in their memorable win over hosts Spain in 1982?

17 Which African nation beat West Germany in 1982?

18 Which Brazilian star smoked 60 cigarettes a day, played the guitar and wrote poetry (not necessarily at the same time)?

19 What was England's dreadful mascot in Spain?

20 Which of the following played in World Cup final tournaments – Rodney Marsh, Alfredo di Stefano, George Best?

QUIZ 11

WHO'S WHO 1

Identify the following players from the selective biographical details.

1 London born forward, debut 1974, clubs include Orient, WBA, Real Madrid, Manchester United, Marseilles and Leicester

2 Southampton and the First Division's top scorer in the 1981–82 season

3 Australian born defender whose first league goal was in 1985–86; joined Chelsea from Villa

4 Had the following number of league appearances for Liverpool in successive seasons from 1977: 42, 42, 42, 34, 42, 42, 33, 36

5 Midfielder and Eire international, played for Manchester United, Derby, Coventry, Birmingham and Shrewsbury

6 Defender whose surname includes a 'Z', had at least 16 solid seasons with Blackburn from 1970

7 Born in Marrakesh and played for USM Casablanca, but made his name scoring 13 goals in 1958 World Cup

8 Only 5 ft 8 in tall, known as 'Der Bomber', he was a prolific scorer for club and country in the 1970s

9 First league club Scunthorpe in 1965. By 1987, made a record 42nd appearance at Wembley when appeared in goal in the FA Cup final

10 A UEFA Cup final team comprising Redford, Holt, Narey, Thomson, Hegarty, Bannon, Malpas, Kirkwood, McInally, Sturrock and Bowman

11 Top scorer in Division Two 1958–59 and 1959–60, playing for Middlesbrough. Now top manager

12 Algerian international, played for Crystal Palace and QPR in late seventies before joining Notts County

13 Sunderland born striker whose clubs have been Lincoln, Newcastle, Bristol City, Birmingham and Luton

14   Early league club rejections, two spells in Canada and a £1.9 million transfer fee to his name

15   1098 appearances in first class football

16   Despite a fractured skull in 1972, went on to make over 600 league and cup appearances for Celtic

17   Forenames 'William Ralph' but this phenomenal goalscorer was better known by his nickname at Goodison Park

18   The oldest footballer to play in Division One when five days over 50

19   Originally with Spurs for three seasons without playing, joined Middlesbrough and subsequently Liverpool, Sampdoria and Rangers

20   Became QPR's most expensive ever signing when he joined in February 1989

QUIZ 12

FORWARD THINKING

The following questions are all about goalscorers.

1   Which Southampton striker was the First Division's leading goalscorer in 1979–80?

2   Which Ajax forward won the Golden Boot award for being Europe's leading scorer in 1985–86?

3   Which Ipswich player became the first Briton to score three penalties in one European game in 1980?

4   Joe Payne holds the record for the most goals in a league game in Britain – how many?

5   What was Pat Kruse's achievement in 6 seconds whilst playing for Torquay *v.* Cambridge in 1977?

6   Who has scored more league goals for Tottenham than anybody else?

7   Who achieved the prolific scoring rate of 68 goals in 62 appearances for his country between 1966 and 1974?

8   Who was the first Briton to be awarded the Golden Boot?

9 Who scored in every game for Brazil in the 1970 World Cup?

10 Who was the first player to score 100 goals in both the Scottish and English leagues?

11 Francis Lee scored 33 goals in the First Division in 1971–72. Who was the next player to reach 30 in one season?

12 Who was Aston Villa's top scorer when they won the league in 1980–81?

13 Who scored 42 of Bournemouth's 81 league goals in 1970–71?

14 Who were Holland's two scorers in the 1988 European Championship final?

15 Name either of the two Italian clubs that Joe Jordan played for.

16 Whose prolific scoring earned him the 1987 Player of the Year award?

17 Who is the only player to score five goals in an international for England since the war?

18 Which striker of the 1950s scored six goals on his debut for Newcastle?

19 Who came from St Mirren and scored 26 league goals in his first season in England?

20 Four FA Cup finals in the 1970s finished 1–0. Name the heroes.

QUIZ 13

OUTSIDE THE BOX

The following set of questions are a mixed bag and of no particular theme.

1 Which of the following have never played in the Football League – Bob Scorer, Tony Pass or Norman Corner?

2 For the 1987–88 season in England, the average Division One attendance was less than 20 000. True or false?

3 . . . And the Second Division less than 10 000. True or false?

4 Who was the only Liverpool player to appear in all the club's European Cup final wins?

5 The supporters of which Scottish club were awarded the FIFA Fair Play trophy of 1987?

6 Which contemporary England centre back was born in Singapore?

7 Which was the first country to defeat England after their World Cup victory, beating them 3–2 at Wembley?

8 Which club was originally known as Ardwick FC?

9 'United have just got the bargain of all time, and I am not at all happy.' About whose transfer fee, fixed by tribunal, was Billy McNeill talking?

10 Which two clubs contested the first all-British European final?

11 Which was the second club to achieve the league and FA Cup double, after Preston?

12 Who achieved the more unusual double of league and League Cup in the 1970s, the first club to do so?

13 Which member of the Royal Family is the President of the FA?

14 Where was the 1986 World Cup due to be staged?

15 Which country won the last British International Championship to be held, in 1984?

16 Who won the Littlewoods Cup in 1988?

17 What were the European Championships formerly known as?

18 Which of the four home countries won the 1988 Victory Shield for Under-15s?

19 Name the three league clubs beginning with 'D'.

20 At which ground is the annual Oxford – Cambridge university game held?

QUIZ 14

SCOTTISH FOOTBALL 1

1 Which Hearts player became, in 1980, the first Scottish footballer to be awarded the OBE?

2 Who wrote Scotland's classic 1982 World Cup song, 'We Have a Dream'?

3 Who did B&Q replace as sponsors of the Scottish League?

4 In which year was the Premier Division first contested – 1973, 1975 or 1977?

5 What 'first' occurred in the October 1987 Skol Cup final?

6 Who is the Secretary of the Scottish League?

7 Which team, after Rangers and Celtic, has won the cup most times?

8 From which club did Pat Nevin join Chelsea?

9 Who has been Aberdeen's most capped player?

10 Name the four players charged with 'conduct likely to produce a breach of the peace' following the October 1987 Rangers – Celtic game

11 Name either of Celtic's scorers in their 1967 European Cup final win?

12 Who were runners-up to Celtic at the end of the 1987–88 season?

13 Which is the only Scottish club to have won the European Super Cup?

14 Which full back made 62 appearances for the national side during 16 seasons at Celtic?

15 What was Frank McGarvey's club before he joined Celtic in the 1979–80 season?

16 Which club resigned from the Scottish League in 1967?

17 Which club is the older, Rangers or Celtic?

18 Which Spanish club did Ted McMinn join after leaving Rangers?

19 Who was the Aberdeen striker who was third in the Golden Boot table in 1972?

20 Which club reached the semi-finals of the European Cup in 1956 and the Fairs Cup in 1961?

QUIZ 15

BEAT THE INTRO 1

From the following selected details, identify the player or club as soon as possible – you don't have to wait until the end of the question.

1 Born in Mozambique in 1942, was the first African footballer to make a world reputation . . . International Sports Personality of the Year in 1966 . . . Made debut for Portugal after just 21 games for Benfica

2 Ground capacity 26 812, formed 1905 . . . Nickname is that of a bird . . . Runners-up twice in the League Cup in the 1970s, winners 1985 . . . Recent managers include Ron Saunders and John Bond

3 First £100 a week player in England . . . Played for just one club side – over 700 games – without winning any honours, but also had 52 caps for England . . . Famous Fulham No. 10

4 Real name Francisco Ernami Lima da Silva . . . One-time bricklayer's apprentice . . . Late developer at international level, became the first player from his country to play in the Football League in 1987

5 Had trials for Huddersfield in the mid-1950s as a bespectacled youngster . . . First team at 16 . . . Became Scotland's youngest ever international in 1958 . . . 55 caps over 16 years, 50 goals . . . BBC Radio expert

6 He has a Surinamese father and a Dutch mother . . . Clubs include Feyenoord and PSV Eindhoven . . . One of only two Dutchmen to be European Footballer of the Year . . . Since departed to the Italian league, a fee reported at £5.5 million

7 Played his last match aged 50 . . . But pre-dated Stanley Matthews by 40 years, making debut for Man City in 1894 . . . Always played with a toothpick in his mouth

. . . Played for United, City and 48 times for Wales, which remained a record for over 40 years

8   Team managed by an ex-Newcastle stalwart, who brought in fellow ex-pros Pop Robson and John Craggs to his staff . . . Play at the Victoria Ground . . . Brian Clough began his managerial career at this Fourth Division club

9   First Division footballer with four 'A' levels . . . Midfielder who began his career at Reading . . . Only four league goals in 1987–88 season, but one vital Cup one . . . Self-confessed 'The Cup-winning goalscorer no one can remember'

10   He was the youngest player to make his First Division debut for Everton . . . A centre forward who moved to Manchester, and ended his playing career in East Anglia . . . Manager of North West Division Two side since 1982

QUIZ 16

MORE QUOTES

1   Complete the following Bill Shankly quote: 'There are two great teams on Merseyside, . . .'

2   Which former Leeds and Everton striker did John Toshack describe, 'He's like a motor car. Six owners and been in the garage most of the time'?

3   'I thought the number 10, Whymark, played exceptionally well,' said Mrs Thatcher after the 1978 FA Cup final. Why was her remark flawed?

4   'We don't use a stopwatch to judge our golden goal competition now. We use a calendar.' Which club's goal famine was Tommy Docherty describing in 1985?

5   'The Pope may be Polish, but God is _____'?

6   'Devonshire's the cream, Rice is the pudding.' When was this banner seen?

7   Who said, 'There are more hooligans in the House of Commons than at a football match'?

8   'Mind, I've been here during the bad times too. One year we came second.' Which club was being described?

9 'Imagine Franz Beckenbauer trying to play for them. He'd just be in the way.' Which club was Frank McLintock talking about in 1982?

10 What song lyric precedes, 'His knees have all gone trembly'?

11 'You lose some. You draw some.' Which comedian described Birmingham thus?

12 Who did Roy Hattersley describe as 'nobody's friends except when there are FA Cup final tickets to give away'?

13 'The Chairman, Doug Ellis, said he was right behind me.' Who replied, 'I'd sooner have him in front of me where I can see him'?

14 'If we go all the way to Wembley, it's difficult to imagine the club looking elsewhere for a new manager.' Who was sacked despite Chairman Mike Bamber's prediction?

15 Who said, in 1967, 'I'm no angel, but I've never kicked anyone deliberately'?

16 Who coined the expression, 'It only takes a second to score a goal'?

17 Who said, on the eve of his debut in England in 1983, 'Looking back, some of the pictures I've posed for have been daft'?

18 'I've heard of players selling dummies, but this club keeps buying them', said Len Shackleton. Which club?

19 'I don't drop players, I make changes'. Who said this?

20 From which TV series does the following line come: 'Funny you should mention that about footballers, Oz, because the only older woman I ever had looked like Billy Bremner'?

QUIZ 17

SING WHEN YOU'RE WINNING

The following questions all refer to that rather uneasy relationship, football and pop music.

1   Which is the only football team record to have reached number one?

2   Who released 'Ole Ola' in anticipation of Scotland's 1978 World Cup campaign?

3   At which London ground did The Who play in the 1970s?

4   What was the result of the Housemartins' first LP?

5   What was the name of the song recorded for Sport Aid by 'The Football Managers'?

6   What was England's classic song for the 1982 World Cup?

7   Which London side does Julian Lloyd Webber support enthusiastically?

8   Who is Torquay's manager, once immortalized in a pop song?

9   Which musical duo of the 1970s, who had a number one hit with 'Welcome Home', might have come from the England football team?

10   Half Man Half Biscuit recorded a song with what unusual request as its title?

11   Which member of the Skids was once on Dunfermline's books?

12   'Was I the fifth Beatle? No, what they meant was I wasn't your average don't-do-anything-till-Saturday footballer'. Who said this?

13   Which actor featured on Scotland's 1982 World Cup song?

14   Which top manager once sang with the Joe Loss Orchestra?

15   Which club does DJ John Peel support vociferously?

16   The B side of 'Back Home' is which of the following – 'On The Way', 'Mexico Bound' or 'Cinnamon Stick'?

17   'Blue Is The Colour' and 'Ossie's Dream' both reached the same position in the British pop charts – what was it?

18   With whom did Nottingham Forest record their effort, 'We've Got the Whole World in our Hands'?

19   What was the title of Glenn and Chris' hit single?

20   Who wrote the hit 'Anfield Rap'?

QUIZ 18

MINOR LEAGUE

1   The average attendance in the GM Vauxhall Conference for the 1987–88 season was above or below 1000?

2   Which (then) Gola League side reached the final of the Welsh Cup in 1986?

3   Which side won the 1988 FA Trophy?

4   Which former league club was relegated from the Northern Premier League in 1988?

5   In which league do Croydon play?

6   Which club recorded a gate of over 6000 in the Vauxhall-Opel league in 1988?

7   Who was the Sutton manager who described football as a 'harsh mistress' after his side's FA Cup run ended in an 8–0 defeat at Norwich?

8   Name any of the three top scorers in the GM Vauxhall Conference in the 1987–88 season.

9   . . . Who finished runners-up to Lincoln in that season?

10   When Lincoln won the GM Vauxhall Conference in 1988, which team were the top goal scorers?

11   Nottingham Forest won the FA Cup in 1959, but which South London amateur side came within a whisker of beating them in the Third Round?

12   Who was Frank Worthington playing for in the 1988–89 season?

13   Name any of the three sides that Charlton manager Lennie Lawrence played for.

14   Which league do Ovenden Papers sponsor?

15   Sutton United beat Coventry in the FA Cup in 1989, but which (now) First Division team did they take to a replay the previous season?

16 Dave Beasant, subject of the largest fee ever paid for a goalkeeper, originally joined Wimbledon for £1000. From which club?

17 Who was the 1988 Players' Player of the Year in the GMVC?

18 Against whom did England play their one semi-professional international in the 1987–88 season?

19 Which side appeared in three FA Trophy finals in succession, 1985–87?

20 Who were the Welsh Cup holders who defeated Atalanta in the first leg of the Cup Winners Cup in 1988?

QUIZ 19

CAPTAINS

1 In which year did England captain Bryan Robson make his international debut?

2 Who captained Argentina's 1978 World Cup winning side?

3 Which captain of Worcestershire County Cricket Club also skippered Lincoln in 1982–83?

4 Who was the captain of the brilliant 1970 Brazilian team?

5 Who was the last goalkeeper to captain an FA Cup winning team?

6 Which Rangers skipper played his last international in 1976 after 44 caps?

7 Which side did Jimmy Dixon captain to a record seventh FA Cup in 1957?

8 Who was the Argentinian captain sent off *v.* England in 1966, the first player to be dismissed at Wembley?

9 Bill Shankly told a story of the 1966 Cup final in which Princess Margaret's response to the question where is Everton, and being told it was in Liverpool, was 'Of course, we had your first team here last year'. Who was the Everton captain addressed?

10 Who captained Holland to the 1988 European Championships title?

11 Who became the youngest ever captain of an FA Cup final side in 1969?

12 Which clubs did the following captain in 1977 – Martin Peters, Dave Watson, John Hollins?

13 Who was captain of the Aston Villa team when they last won the league, in 1981?

14 Who was the last captain to lift the FA Cup twice in succession?

15 Who was the club captain of Mansfield who was elevated to player-manager after the dismissal of Ian Greaves in 1989?

16 Which actor played the lead role in the 1982 TV drama, *The World Cup: A Captain's Tale?*

17 Who was the captain of the Brazil side at the 1982 World Cup?

18 Which 1980s captain of Liverpool played volleyball and golf at junior international level?

19 Which player of 100 caps led Wolves in the 1949 FA Cup final?

20 This captain created a record in international matches by keeping a clean sheet for 1142 minutes between September 1972 and June 1974. Who is he?

QUIZ 20

GEOGRAPHY TEST 1 - UK

Solve the following clues and match them to the numbers on the map.

A The birth place of Bryan Robson; **B** The Cobblers play their home games here; **C** Town in which you'd find Meadowbank Thistle; **D** University Brian McClair attended as a 19-year-old chemistry student; **E** The last club before Liverpool to retain the League Cup; **F** The team that John Arlott used to cycle 16 miles each way to see; **G** Peter Beardsley's first club; **H** Home is Home Park; **I** They are found at Gay Meadow; **J** Club which prompted Tommy

Docherty to say in 1985, 'I just opened the trophy cabinet. Two Japanese prisoners of war jumped out'; **K** Club where Kenny Dalglish spent two weeks on trial from Celtic in 1966; **L** Club that Moroccan Mohammed Ali-Amar joined on loan in 1989.

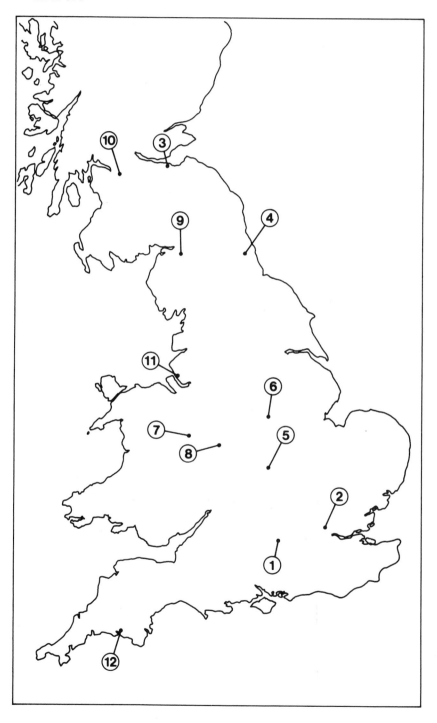

PICTURE QUIZ 2

IDENTIFICATION PARADE

1   Which national side is this?

2   Where would you find this pre-match lesson?

3   Shooting practice . . . who is it?

4   Which trophy is this?

QUIZ 21

RAPID FIRE

These questions are 'fingers on the buzzer' type.

1 Alphabetically, which league club follows Fulham?

2 Who won the World Cup in 1982?

3 Who is the other half of John Sillett's successful managerial partnership?

4 Who succeeded Don Revie as England manager?

5 For which club did Jimmy Armfield appear 568 times?

6 Who has won more caps for Wales than anyone else?

7 Who was Scotland's manager at the 1986 World Cup?

8 Which was Pele's first World Cup?

9 Which team did Howard Kendall leave Everton to manage?

10 How many days did Brian Clough last at Leeds?

11 Who has been capped most times for England?

12 Who was manager of Arsenal immediately before George Graham?

13 Where do Bury play?

14 Who scored a record seven goals for Arsenal v. Aston Villa in 1935?

15 Which club went 31 games without a victory during the 1983–84 season?

16 Which keeper established a British record of maintaining a clean sheet for 1196 minutes, November 1986–January 1987?

17 To the nearest year, how old was Norman Whiteside when he made his debut for Northern Ireland?

18 Who overtook Terry Paine's record of 824 league appearances?

19 England have never played Egypt. True or false?

20 Which is the highest division that Hereford have played in?

QUIZ 22

RECORD BREAKERS

1   Celtic, CSKA Sofia and MTK Budapest share the record for the most successive national league championships – how many?

2   How many first class matches did it take Pele to notch up 1000 goals – 909, 999 or 1117?

3   Which club, formed in 1861, is the oldest still in the league?

4   What did Jimmy Scarth achieve in 2½ minutes for Gillingham *v.* Orient in a league match in 1952?

5   Who is the Republic of Ireland's most capped player?

6   Which side remained unbeaten for 42 consecutive league matches, November 1977–December 1978?

7   Which club has won the Welsh Cup most times?

8   The European tie between Celtic and Leeds in 1970 attracted a record crowd. Was it 95 000, 115 000 or 135 000?

9   How many seasons did it take Wimbledon to go from the Southern League to the First Division?

10   In 14 seasons to 1987, how many times did Liverpool appear at Wembley – 10, 14 or 19?

11   Who has scored most hat-tricks in a league season since the war?

12   Who has the stunning record of scoring 85 goals in 84 games for Hungary?

13   Who was 38 years 2 months when he made his debut for England in 1950?

14   What was Bury's unique distinction in winning the FA Cup in 1903?

15   Which Brazilian, a member of the 1970 side, has a national record of 120 caps?

16   In which town was the first football club founded?

17   Who is the most capped British player?

18 Who is the most successful manager in the history of the Football League?

19 What is the furthest round a Fourth Division side has reached in the FA Cup?

20 Which European nation has won most European club competitions?

QUIZ 23

GROUNDS

1 Which ground did Bobby Charlton describe as 'a theatre of dreams'?

2 Which ground houses the Bob Lord stand?

3 Chesterfield and Aldershot's grounds have the same name – what is it?

4 Which European capital has the 23 August stadium?

5 Which club is known as 'The Academy of Football' and what is the official name of its ground?

6 What was unusual about the venue of the Wales – Scotland World Cup game in 1981?

7 In whose ground was the Braemar Stand gutted by fire in 1983?

8 Which European club play at the Estadio da Lux, or Stadium of Light?

9 Which club once played in West Bromwich Road?

10 At which ground is there a gate with the words 'You'll Never Walk Alone' above it?

11 Which three London grounds are owned by Marler Estates?

12 Which ground witnessed the first major tragedy, during a Scotland – England international in 1902?

13 Which was the first club to open a creche at its ground?

14 Where would you find the Paxton end?

15 The FGIT was set up in 1975. What does FGIT stand for?

16 In March 1946, 33 people died and 400 were injured after a crush at which English ground?

17 If a Littlewoods Cup match over two legs was played at Brunton Park and Feethams, which two clubs would be playing?

18 Arsenal have the Clock End, but where would you find the Clock Stand?

19 Which major club has a Kop apart from Liverpool?

20 Which league venue was once a Test cricket ground?

QUIZ 24

HAPPY FAMILIES

1 Height 6 ft 2 in, date of birth 25.9.56; height 6 ft 0 in, date of birth 25.9.56. Identify.

2 Of which footballing dynasty is Bradley of QPR the latest addition?

3 The former manager of Brazil, Edu, is the elder brother of which star?

4 Which brothers scored for opposite sides in a league match between Wolves and Newcastle in 1975?

5 How did Southampton make post-war history in October 1988?

6 Who were the Chilean brothers who played for Newcastle in the 1952 FA Cup final?

7 Frank, Derek, Allan, Kelvin and Wayne have all played league football. What is the family name?

8 At which club, previously associated with his father, has Chris McMenemy been appointed coach?

9 Four MacLaren brothers were with league clubs in the 1950s; what was the position that they all shared?

10 The 38 year old son of a famous manager was appointed coach at Burnley in 1989 – who is he?

11 141 caps for England in the family. Whose?

12 Two brothers Leslie and Dennis played in the Arsenal

cup winning side of 1950. Dennis was noted for even greater achievements in another sport. Who are they?

13   Which two Norwich managers of the last 15 years have included their sons in their teams?

14   His brother has captained England, but not at football. He played at Wembley for Brighton. Who is he?

15   Mel is the less famous of two brothers who played in the same team for Wales. John was better known. What is the family name?

16   George, Jack and Jim played for Leeds. Stan played for Chesterfield, Rochdale and Leicester. What is the legendary family name?

17   A current international centre forward's father was the top scorer in the 1965 League Cup, for Aston Villa. Who are the father and son?

18   Alan was a favourite at Upton Park in the 1960s. Les is a contemporary Luton goalkeeper. Who are they?

19   Bill Dodgin Senior and Bill Dodgin Junior both had spells managing which London club?

20   He was born in Sunderland and made his league debut in 1984–85. His father played twice for England while at Middlesbrough. Who is he?

QUIZ 25

TEAM SHEETS

Each of these famous line-ups has two players missing. You have to identify them.

1   Manchester United – 1968 European Cup Final
Stepney, Brennan, Dunne, ..., Foulkes, Stiles, Best, Kidd, Charlton, Sadler, ...

2   Brazil – 1970 World Cup Final
Felix, Carlos Alberto, Brito, Piazza, Everaldo, Gerson, Clodoaldo, Jairzinho, Pele, ...,
. . . .

3   Sunderland – 1973 FA Cup Final
Montgomery, Malone, Guthrie, Horswill,
. . . ., Pitt, Kerr, Hughes, Halom, Porterfield,
. . . .

4   England – 1966 World Cup Final (inevitably)
    Banks, ..., Wilson, Stiles, Charlton,
    Moore, ..., Hurst, Charlton, Hunt, Peters.

5   Tottenham – 1982 FA Cup Final
    Clemence, Hughton, Miller, Price, Hazard (Brooke),
    Perryman, Roberts, ..., Galvin,
    . . . ., Crooks.
    Clue: both played on the Continent

6   Scotland – v. West Germany, 1986 World Cup, Mexico
    . . . ., Gough, Malpas, ...,
    Narey, Miller, Strachan, Aitken, Nicol, Archibald,
    Bannon.

7   England – v. France, 1982 World Cup, Bilbao
    Shilton, Mills, Sansom (Neal), ..., Butcher,
    Robson, Coppell, Wilkins, ..., Francis,
    Rix.

8   Arsenal – 1971 FA Cup Final
    Wilson, Rice, McNab, Storey (Kelly), ...,
    Simpson, Armstrong, ..., Radford,
    Kennedy, George.

9   West Germany – 1974 World Cup Final
    . . . ., Vogts, Schwarzenbeck, Beckenbauer,
    Breitner, Bonhof, Hoeness, ..., Grabowski,
    Muller, Holzenbein.

10 England – v. Scotland, 1974, Glasgow
    Shilton, ..., ..., Hughes,
    Hunter, Todd, Channon, Bell, Worthington
    (Macdonald), Weller, Peters.

QUIZ 26

BEFORE & AFTER

Given the event and year, you have to fill in the predecessor
and successor.

PREDECESSOR	NAME	EVENT	YEAR	SUCCESSOR
1	Sheffield Wednesday	FA Cup runners-up	1966	. . . .
2	Jimmy Armfield	Leeds managers	–	. . . .
3	Aberdeen	Scottish League Premier champions	1984	. . . .

QUIZ 27

SOCCER & POLITICS

1 Who, in 1987, dedicated his European Footballer of the Year award to Nelson Mandela?

2 Which former England captain was quoted in 1980 as saying 'I have never voted anything but Labour in my life. And I never will'?

3 Which former Labour MP bought a football club in January 1982?

4 Who said, 'I know more about politics than I do about football'?

5 Who was behind the campaign to abolish the maximum wage in football?

6 Which judge was responsible for reporting on the findings from the enquiries into the Bradford fire and Birmingham riots?

7 'The politics involved made me nostalgic for the Middle East'. Who said this, after FIFA rejected the USA bid to stage the 1986 World Cup?

8 What connection is there between a Millwall winger and a former US President?

9 Roland Boyes MP is a director and lifelong supporter of which North East club?

10 Two players, since managers, Steve Coppell and Brian Talbot, are both former chairmen of what organization?

11 Who wrote in his book *Goodbye to Yorkshire*, 'As a boy I genuinely believed in the man who never ate bacon because its red and white stripes reminded him of Sheffield United'?

12 Before the laws of the game were re-organized last century, how many monarchs had banned football in one form or another – 0, 1 or 4?

13 Who was the Minister of Sport at the time when England won the World Cup in 1966?

14 Which Prime Minister later said, 'Have you noticed how we only win the World Cup under a Labour government?'?

15 And which Minister recorded in his diaries, 'England's victory could be a decisive factor in strengthening sterling'?

16 What was the name of the legislation that proposed national identity cards for all club supporters?

17 In which year was UEFA formed – 1934, 1954 or 1969?

18 Which Brazilian replaced Sir Stanley Rous as President of FIFA in 1974?

19 What is the name of the Tory MP who is Chairman of Luton?

20 Which country was being described by Ted Croker when he said, 'Football is primarily a black man's game there . . . but unfortunately they have no black competitions'?

QUIZ 28

THE SEVENTIES

All the questions in this section refer to the period 1970–79.

1 Who, in 1978, became the first black player to play for England?

2 How many FA Cup finals went to replays during the decade?

3 Which club joined the Scottish League in 1974?

4   How many teams won the league twice?

5   In which year did Alf Ramsey cease to be England manager?

6   Which minor league side defeated Burnley in the Third Round of the FA Cup in 1975 before losing to Leeds after a replay?

7   Which club achieved the unusual double of League Cup and Cup Winners Cup in 1970?

8   For which two clubs did the final match of the 1975–76 season have a critical outcome?

9   No London team won the league during the decade – true or false?

10 Three Brazilians won the title South American Footballer of the Year in the seventies – name two of them.

11 . . . Name either the Peruvian or the Argentinian who also won it.

12 Who won the Cup Winners Cup in 1972, beating Moscow Dynamo 3–2 in the final?

13 Which former Wolves manager became national coach of Saudi Arabia in the mid-seventies?

14 In which year did the Bishop of Norwich have occasion to write to *The Times* arguing against Sunday football?

15 Who was transferred from Hereford to Brighton and scored just 50 seconds into his league debut in March 1976?

16 Which Third Division side reached the semi-finals of the FA Cup in 1976?

17 Name three of the four clubs for whom Ted MacDougall and Phil Boyer played together?

18 In a First Division game in March 1976, Chris Nicholl scored all four goals in a 2–2 draw with Norwich. Who for?

19 Which team gained election to the league in 1970?

20 Which London club's players volunteered to take a cut in wages in July 1976?

QUIZ 29

BRITISH FOOTBALL 2

1   The following have all played in the Football League, true or false – Steve Death, Keith Fear, Geoff Coffin?

2   Who was the Wolves defender who left the club to become a Jehovah's witness?

3   Who was the Football Writers Player of the Year for the 1987–88 season?

4   Name either of the sides who have won the Second Division a record six times.

5   Who was relegated from the league when Lincoln gained automatic promotion at the end of the 1988 season?

6   Only three league clubs begin with the letter R. Name them.

7   Which league side has Ian Botham played for?

8   Which match takes place between the Eagles and the Seagulls?

9   Who was voted in as Football League President (for the second time) in November 1988?

10 Who was the Football Writers Player of the Year in 1947–48 and then again 15 years later?

11 In the play-offs at the end of the 1987–88 season, how many of the three higher division sides avoided relegation?

12 . . . Who were runners-up to Liverpool in the league that season?

13 . . . And who was the Young Player of the Year?

14 Which Second Division club has the largest non-season ticket membership scheme in the Football League, with over 35 000 members?

15 Which club was once known as Thames Ironworks FC?

16 Who did Wigan replace in the league when elected in 1978?

17 Who bowed out in his 500th league game with a goal for Newcastle in 1983?

18 Who finished runners-up in the league in their first season in Division One in 1983?

19 Who was the Republic of Ireland striker dropped for the first time in February 1989 after scoring just one goal in 21 matches?

20 Which of the following has *not* played in the Football League – Mark Graves, Martin Bone or John Skull?

QUIZ 30

A – Z 2

The answer to each question begins with the letter indicated.

A Founder member of the league, no longer playing in it

B 56 caps for Northern Ireland, and led Spurs to the double

C Hosts of the 1962 World Cup

D They play at Boghead Park

E Bristol Rovers had to vacate this ground

F They recorded the biggest win in the history of the European Cup

G Irish side who reached the quarter-finals of the 1974 Cup Winners Cup

H Split team in Yugoslavia

I West Ham's YTS discovery

J Trophy won outright in 1970

K They play at Rugby Park

L Leading Division Two scorer in 1982–83 season

M First Third Division club to reach the FA Cup semi-finals

N Supplier of Cruyff in 1974 World Cup, left Ajax for Barcelona

O They sold Ray Houghton to Liverpool for £825 000

P Edson Arantes di Nascimento

Q British club formerly called St Jude's

R Dutchman who scored the 1000th goal in World Cup finals when converted penalty *v.* Scotland in 1978

S Their first major honour came in 1972

T They play at Plainmoor

U They have appeared in three World Cups

V Wales play some of their home games here

W As a Third Division club, reached League Cup semi-finals in 1984

X Alphabetically, the first English league club to include an X in their name

Y Liverpool centre back of the 1960s, also managed Tranmere

Z Artur Antunes Coimbra

QUIZ 31

MANAGERS 2

The nature of football in the modern era is such that these questions are probably those most subject to becoming outdated.

1 Which club did George Graham manage before Arsenal?

2 Which GM Vauxhall Conference club became Tommy Docherty's 15th managerial position?

3 How many managers have Derby County had since Brian Clough – 3, 5 or 7?

4 Which manager, when his new club were relegated to Division Three in 1988, had been in charge of two relegated sides in the same season?

5 Who was the manager of the Portuguese side Setubal who was banned from the touchline for seven weeks in February 1988?

6 Name either of the former Burnley stars who at the start of 1989 were manager and assistant manager of Bury.

7 At which club has Bobby Gould had two spells as manager?

8   Which manager, despite his club's relegation at the end of the 1988 season, won a league championship medal?

9   Which former Spurs stalwart managed Brentford through their FA Cup run in 1989?

10 Who was the Fourth Division club who sacked their manager Mike Walker while he was 'Manager of the Month'?

11 Chris Turner manages Cambridge; who does his namesake manage?

12 Which much travelled player took on the player-manager's job at Bristol Rovers after David Williams' departure?

13 Name the two former Leeds managers who have also managed home international sides.

14 Three of the 1968 European Cup-winning Manchester United team have since managed Preston. Name two of them.

15 West Bromwich Albion have had four managers with the forename Ron since the war – name three.

16 'After ten years I want to put my reputation on the line again'. Which manager said this in May 1987 after his move to the Midlands?

17 Which Hungarian maestro had a spell managing Panathinaikos?

18 Who was the Manchester United manager lured to take charge of Iran's national side in 1974?

19 Who has won the Manager of the Month award most often?

20 Ian Branfoot won the award in March 1988; unusually he was not a First Division manager. What was his club?

QUIZ 32

FANATICS & FANZINES

The first ten questions are all deliberately difficult, and therefore for the fanatic.

1   Which Spurs player, in the period February 1965 to

October 1966, scored 26 goals in home games and none in away ones?

2 Who missed a penalty with his last kick in English football, thereby condemning Sheffield United to relegation to Division Four for the first time, in 1981?

3 Which club holds the record for the longest stretch in the Third Division, 47 years?

4 Which club finished 14th in Division One four seasons in a row from 1966–67, finishing with points of 39, 38, 39, 39 respectively?

5 Who, in 1989, reached the Fifth Round of the FA Cup for a record eighth successive season?

6 In 1970–71, in how many of Arsenal's 64 games did they keep a clean sheet?

7 In 1989, which minor league side included American international John Kerr and Trinidad & Tobago's goalkeeper, John Granville?

8 Can you make a connection between current league players with first names Keith, Alan and Craig?

9 What landmark of goalscoring did the winners of all four divisions reach in 1956–57?

10 Johnny Giles was on three winning sides in Wembley finals – Manchester United – Leicester (1963 FA Cup), and the Leeds – Arsenal games of the 1968 League Cup and 1972 FA Cup. Which defender was on the losing side each time?

The following list are all titles of club fanzines. If you haven't heard of fanzines yet, you should have. They are the witty, sometimes intelligent alternative voice of football. You have to identify the clubs from which they hail.

11 Brian Moore's Head

12 Elm Park Disease

13 Tired and Weary

14 Bernard of the Bantams

15 King of Kippax

16 Out of Court

17 One Nil Down, Two One Up

18 The Proclaimer

19 When Sunday Comes

20 Sing When We're Fishing

21 Witton Wisdom

22 Flashing Blade

23 The Mag

24 Light at the End of the Tunnel (minor league)

25 Never Mind The Boleyn

QUIZ 33

THE NAME'S THE SAME

A less serious quiz in which the questions are based on common surnames. Some are mildly cryptic.

1 Tom of The Rights of Man and Terry of 700+ appearances.

2 Alan's Jazzmen?

3 'Two . . . . , there's only two . . . .'. To whom were England fans referring in Mexico 1986?

4 Colin, David, Ian, Joe, Paul, Willie?

5 A former British Prime Minister and a Manchester United idol.

6 Johnny of Fulham and Desmond of prolific opening stands?

7 DH and Tommy?

8 Jack Rollin's *Who's Who In Soccer* lists all the players in the English and Scottish leagues. Which was the most common surname, with 23 – Jones, Williams or Smith?

9 Billy, the Palace and Portsmouth defender, and one half of a famous musical duo.

10 Dizzy Gary?

11 Former England striker and TV contributor, and a contemporary Cabinet minister.

12 A former Sunderland midfielder and the Galloping Gourmet.

13 Alan of West Ham falling on Hard Times?

14 Steve's worth £1 million and TV namesake Arthur less so.

15 Charlie Boy?

16 Johnny of Leeds and Bill of TV weather.

17 Alan, 12 seasons at Burnley 1971–83, well known for his rocket?

18 Alan, once of Manchester United, and the kings of football.

19 Athletic Eddie?

20 Ronald and Malcolm.

QUIZ 34

EUROPEAN & INTERNATIONAL 2

1 Who was European Footballer of the Year three years in succession, 1983–85?

2 Which club has more registered fans than any other in Europe?

3 Name the two sides beaten by Nottingham Forest in the 1979 and 1980 finals of the European Cup.

4 In which country do Fluminense play?

5 To whom did Celtic lose in the 1970 European Cup final?

6 Elias Figueroa won the title of South American Footballer of the Year for the third time in succession in 1976. What was his nationality?

7 Who is the all-time leading Italian scorer in European club competitions?

8 Who, in June 1968 against Yugoslavia, became the first England player to be sent off?

9 What was the venue for the 1963 European Cup Final between AC Milan and Benfica?

10 Which Chelsea player, past or present, has most international caps whilst playing for them?

11 To whom did Dundee United lose in the 1987 UEFA Cup final?

12 Which was the first club to win the European Cup on penalties, in 1986?

13 Who played in more Fairs Cup matches, Birmingham or Arsenal?

14 Which country was the first to have clubs represented in all three European club finals – European Cup, Cup Winners Cup and UEFA Cup – in 1986?

15 Italy have never won the European Championships. True or false?

16 The Manchester United air disaster was in 1958, but which Italian club suffered a similar disaster nine years earlier?

17 Which country was banned by FIFA from all international competitions for two years from June 1988 for fielding over-age players in a youth tournament?

18 Who scored Ireland's goal that defeated England in their first match of the 1988 European Championships?

19 . . . Name either of the losing semi-finalists in that tournament.

20 How many times did Martin Chivers play for England in full internationals – 14, 24 or 44?

QUIZ 35

SOCCER & LITERATURE

1 'And life itself is a game of football.' Which prolific 19th century novelist wrote this?

2 What literary French connection do Oran FC of Algeria have?

3 'And I so round with you as you with me
That like a football you do spurn me thus'.
These lines were written in 1590. By whom?

4 Who wrote, 'Football is all very well as a game for rough girls, but it is hardly suitable for delicate boys'?

5   Who wrote the football based novel, *The Blinder*?

6   Whose play, *Professional Foul*, is centred around a philosopher whose real intention in attending a conference in Prague is to catch the Czechoslovakia – England match?

7   Whose autobiography is titled *Paradise Lost* following his dismissal by Celtic?

8   Who was Sutton United's Shakespeare-quoting boss who urged his players, 'Once more unto the breach' at his half-time talk, and who made such an impression on the 1989 FA Cup?

9   From which play was the Norwich chairman's reply, following their 8–0 defeat of Sutton, 'Enough! No more; 'tis not so sweet as it was before'?

10 Which J. B. Priestley novel of 1929 features Bruddersford United, where for a shilling you were offered 'Conflict and Art'?

11 Gordon Williams and Terry Venables co-wrote a futuristic novel in 1971 in which future visions included cantilever stands and plastic pitches. What was it called?

12 In which Alan Bleasdale adaptation does a lead character liken himself to Graeme Souness?

13 Who was the subject of the biography titled *Father of Football*?

14 Which player of the 1950s was described in verse as 'Expressionless enchanter, weaving as on strings'?

15 Which militant Everton fan wrote a book called *Inside Left*?

16 Whose diary recorded in 1665 that 'The streets were full of footballs'?

17 'But I don't see what football has to do with being mayor.' 'You are nothing but a cuckoo – football has to do with everything.'
    In whose book, *The Card*, did this exchange appear?

18 'The delights of the game are mainly these;
    The naked skin to the icy breeze;
    The sting of the rain; the nip of the snow;
    The whip of the wind, that strikes like a blow.'
    From which decade is this extract from *The Boy's Own Annual* taken?

19 Whose autobiographies were a) *Going Great Guns* and b) *Bring on the Clown*?

20 What is the connection between Steve Perryman's autobiography and Thomas More?

QUIZ 36

GOALKEEPERS

1 Which goalkeeper was awarded the MBE in June 1987?

2 Which record-breaking keeper made his debut for Watford in April 1963?

3 For which African side did Kazadi keep goal in the 1974 World Cup?

4 Until when were keepers allowed to handle the ball anywhere in their own half – 1888, 1912 or 1948?

5 Who was the Mexican goalkeeper who played in five consecutive World Cups, 1950–66?

6 Who was the first goalkeeper to save a penalty in an FA Cup final at Wembley?

7 Who was England's goalkeeper in February 1963 for Alf Ramsey's first game as England manager?

8 Who was the Dutch keeper in the 1988 European Championship – he saved a penalty in the final?

9 Which keeper made 73 appearances for England, 37 of them while at Leicester?

10 Name either of the two keepers, apart from Peter Shilton, that Derby had on their books at the beginning of the 1988–89 season.

11 Who was England's keeper for the first 17 internationals after World War Two?

12 Which player – who might have been known as 'The Cat' – played in goal for Brazil in the 1970 World Cup final?

13 What was unusual about Tony Coton's first touch in senior soccer in 1980?

14 Who was Aberdeen's Dutch keeper who made his debut in 1980?

15 Who was in goal for Everton when Jeff Astle scored the winning goal in the 1968 FA Cup final?

16 On which birthday did Pat Jennings celebrate his 119th cap for Northern Ireland?

17 Whose infamous tackle on Battiston left his reputation badly tarnished?

18 Who was the Poland keeper, labelled a 'clown' by Brian Clough, who kept England out of the World Cup in 1973?

19 He was European Footballer of the Year in 1963, and represented The Rest of the World in the FA Centenary match. Who is he?

20 Goalkeeper Li Chan Myung was the unlikely hero of which team in the 1966 World Cup?

QUIZ 37

NICKNAMES

1 What nationality was the goalkeeper dubbed 'Erik the Unready' after his uninspired start for Spurs in 1989?

2 Which World Cup hero was known as 'The Black Panther'?

3 Which club did 'Chopper' Harris manage between November 1984 and June 1985?

4 Which of the following clubs is not nicknamed after a bird – Norwich, Brighton, Rotherham, Wrexham or Sheffield Wednesday?

5 Which manager is known as 'The Bald Eagle'?

6 Which national side is known as the 'Azurri'?

7 Name either of the league clubs known as 'The Latics'.

8 Which Spanish striker is known as 'The Vulture'?

9 Newcastle, 'The Magpies', play at St James' Park. Name either the other league side known as 'The Magpies' or the other side that plays at St James' Park.

10 Name the two teams involved when 'The Railwaymen' play 'The Shaymen'.

11 Which star striker was known as 'The Preston Plumber'?

12 Liam Brady is known as 'Chippy'; did this arise because a) he is a useful carpenter, b) he chips the ball with such skill, or c) his penchant for french fries?

13 Name either of the two English clubs who might have stings in their tails . . .

14 . . . Which Scottish club is known as 'The Wasps'?

15 Crystal Palace are 'The Eagles', but which European club share that nickname?

16 Who is 'Psycho'?

17 Who was the Polish striker of the 1970s affectionately known as 'The Count'?

18 Who were the two Bristol Rovers strikers of the 1970s whose partnership led them to be called 'Smash and Grab'?

19 Whose nickname of 'Banana' prompted the inflatables mania of 1988–89?

20 . . . And whose Cup run led to the fame of 'Harry the Haddock' in February 1989?

QUIZ 38

WORLD CUP 2

1 Not including 1990, how many World Cup tournaments have been staged?

2 How many nations have scored four or more goals in World Cup finals?

3 Which nation scored a shock victory over Italy in 1966 at Ayresome Park?

4 Who was the English referee in charge of the 1974 final between West Germany and Holland?

5 Which of the six previous countries to have won the World Cup were the only ones not to qualify in 1982?

6 Who won FIFA's Fair Play Award in 1986?

7 Who was Denmark's leading scorer in Mexico '86?

8 What colour was Morocco's strip in the last World Cup?

9   Who scored his debut international goal in England's 5–0 defeat of Albania in April 1989?

10 In winning the World Cup in Mexico, Argentina failed to win just one game – against whom?

11 Which England player was sent off in Mexico?

12 . . . And who were the two losing semi-finalists?

13 Who held the record for the youngest player to appear in the World Cup finals before Norman Whiteside?

14 Who was the last player to score twice in a World Cup final?

15 To the nearest 10 000, what was the crowd at the 1950 final between Brazil and Uruguay?

16 Which was the last World Cup to be decided after extra time?

17 Out of the 34 matches England have played in World Cup matches, how many have they won – 15, 19 or 24?

18 Which nation achieved a record score in the final stages by beating El Salvador 10–1 in 1982?

19 Name the two sides who scored six goals in one game at the 1986 Mexico tournament.

20 Which World Cup was Pele describing when he said 'The World Cup cannot be won by toughness'?

PICTURE QUIZ 3

FINDERS KEEPERS

Identify the four goalkeepers.

1

2

3

4

QUIZ 39

GEOGRAPHY TEST 2 - EUROPE

Solve the following clues and match them to the numbers on the map.

A 1987 Italian champions; **B** Club sides B93 and B1903 play in this town; **C** England played here in February 1989; **D** Home of the Bernabeu Stadium; **E** Home of the 1987 European Cup winners; **F** 1988 West German Cup winners; **G** Town with club sides Dinamo and Steaua; **H** Home of club managed by Dino Zoff; **I** Club that Mo Johnston joined from Celtic; **J** Club side Sparta who did the domestic double in 1988.

QUIZ 40

BEAT THE INTRO 2

From the selected details, identify the player or club as soon as possible – you don't have to wait until the end of the question.

1   Born in Ramsgate in 1965 . . . 6 ft 4 in defender . . . His career in the North East included a spell on loan to Darlington . . . In March 1988 became the first Second Division player to be included in the England squad since Peter Taylor in 1976.

2   Their ground capacity is 36 585, though their record attendance is 68 386 . . . Last major honour in 1969, in Europe . . . Won FA Cup in 1955 . . . Have sold a succession of major stars in recent years, including a record British transfer.

3   Player-manager who still occasionally plays, though 'I need 10 minutes notice to score now' . . . Succeeded an ex-teammate at his South West club . . . Former Scotland centre forward, nicknamed 'Fangs' after a 1978 beer commercial.

4   Club that has the following players in common – Gallego, Stieleke, Butragueno . . . 1985 UEFA Cup champions . . . Also Gento, Puskas, Cunningham . . . Complete European domination in early 1960s . . . Also Tendillo, Gordillo, Sanchez.

5   Succeeded Dixie Dean at Everton . . . 66 goals in 87 games up to the war . . . Joined Chelsea, and then Notts County for a record Third Division fee of £20 000 . . . 22 goals in 23 appearances for England in peace time.

6   Founder member of the league, relegated from Division One in 1984 . . . Four times FA Cup winners . . . Managers include Brian Little, Tommy Docherty and Sammy Chapman . . . An average home attendance of 9854 in winning Division Four in 1988.

7   Liverpool apprentice but peripatetic full back . . . Top flight clubs include Villa, Everton and both Manchester clubs . . . One cap for England . . . in 1989 became assistant manager of Darlington, joining former teammate Brian Little.

8   Billy Bingham once managed this club, who play at
    Field Mill . . . They won the Freight Rover Trophy in
    1986–87 . . . Nickname The Stags . . . Ian Greaves was a
    recent manager.

9   Former Dundee United goalkeeper, who began
    managerial career at neighbouring Dens Park . . . Came
    south and managed Coventry until April 1986 . . . Had a
    spell at Rangers helping Graeme Souness, then moved to
    Blackburn in February 1987.

10 Managers include Frank O'Farrell, Jimmy Bloomfield,
    Frank McLintock . . . City replaced their previous name
    Fosse . . . Last in Division One in 1987 . . . FA Cup
    final 1969 . . . Managers include Jock Wallace, Gordon
    Milne, Bryan Hamilton.

QUIZ 41

CRYPTIC CORNER

Perhaps apologies should be made in advance for some of the
following . . .

1   The cleanest Dutch side?

2   This winger might have been married to Everton in the
    early 1970s . . .

3   Football ground battle?

4   Where the Royal Family might watch Northern Ireland
    play?

5   French goalkeeper Joel, who sounds mad?

6   You'd need a spade and an overgrown garden to
    identify this Brighton keeper . . .

7   Former American President Eric?

8   *Name* the connection, apart from Arsenal, between
    Charlie and Graham.

9   Philosophical Brazilian captain?

10 A rolling stone would fail to gather Ernie . . .

11 Birmingham's home University?

12 Alan, Tommy, Dennis, manager Jim?

13 20 Football Yearbooks?

14 Would he only attract supporters when his side were doing well?

15 Always heavy, this First Division side . . .

16 They goosed Coventry at Gander Green Lane . . .

17 Eau de FC?

18 To identify this French international, you might *resort* to an anagram?

19 Perambulating Clive?

20 Well read England full back?

QUIZ 42

WHO'S WHO 2

Identify the following personalities from the selected biographical details.

1 Manager who said, 'I'm not giving away secrets like that to Milan. If I had my way I wouldn't even tell them the time of the kick-off'.

2 Manchester City full back who shared the 1969 Footballer of the Year award with Dave Mackay.

3 He appeared in a record eight championship winning teams with Liverpool before joining Bolton in 1985.

4 A left winger who served under the following managers – Allison (twice), Venables, Whalley, Kember, Gradi, Mullery, Coppell, Pleat, Ball, Bremner and Wilkinson.

5 Centre back for club and country, he missed only six league games for Luton in eight seasons, 1978–86.

6 Arsenal apprentice in 1973 who joined Juventus for £600 000 and returned to London via Sampdoria, Internazionale and Ascoli.

7 Manager of West Germany for 14 years, becoming in that time the most successful manager in the history of the World Cup and European Championships.

8 A Glasgow born defender, he joined Barnsley in the

1985/6 season after serving Birmingham, Forest, Leeds and Derby.

9   League debut for York, and by 1979 the most prolific scorer still active in the league via clubs including Norwich, West Ham and Manchester United.

10 Also a Jimmy, he followed Jimmy Armfield at Leeds.

11 First managed Colchester, then Blackburn, Birmingham, Oxford . . . in 1986 enrolled in the 92 Club for travelling to every ground in the league.

12 A succession of clubs for this striker from Huddersfield to Stockport including Leeds and Sunderland, he played in England's 1989 Veteran side in Brazil for the over-35s.

13 Real Madrid defender who is Spain's most capped player.

14 South Africa born, he has played in the United States but was sold by Chelsea for a bargain £70 000 to Luton.

15 Former Sheffield United and Leeds striker, he is currently the player with the most league goals still playing.

16 361 league appearances in 10 years for Manchester United, and 137 goals, yet still said by some to have cracked up.

17 Victor of a 'Find a Young Player' competition for Liverpool in the 1970s, he never established himself at Anfield, but still has over 200 league goals, most recently at Plymouth.

18 Probably the only Romeo in the history of the league.

19 Sales director, Yorkshireman, referee, took charge of the 1981 FA Cup final, first name Keith.

20 Barcelona's 'errant genius', originally with Cologne, moved on to Real Madrid.

QUIZ 43

DISCIPLINE & SCANDAL

1   For what were nine Wimbledon players each fined £750 in 1988?

2   What ignominious first was achieved by Dave Wagstaffe of Wolves in 1976?

3   Which goalscoring hero of the 1982 World Cup had just returned from a two year ban following a bribes scandal?

4   Why were Luton banned from the 1986 Littlewoods Cup?

5   'Try telling Pat Jennings it was fixed.' What occasioned Billy Bingham to say this?

6   Who drove himself to gaol in 1988?

7   A scandal in which 31 former players and coaches were charged with tax fraud occurred at a club in which European country in January 1989?

8   In which decade were 23 fans arrested for attacking the referee at a Leeds – West Brom game?

9   Name any of the three players imprisoned after a betting ring to fix matches in 1964.

10   For how many games was Paul Davis banned following his televised punching of Glenn Cockerill?

11   Who was sent home from the 1978 World Cup and banned from playing again for his country?

12   'This is the worst thing that has happened in my seven years as manager'. To what incident was Alf Ramsey referring in 1970?

13   In 1986, which country's World Cup squad banned eight players for life following a pay dispute?

14   Which England player managed to collect three yellow cards during the 1986 World Cup?

15   Who was the Spaniard who failed a drugs test at the same competition?

16   In which town did England play Holland in the 1988 European Championships, scene of the supporters' disturbances?

17   Which minor league club's manager, Dogan Arif, was arrested for alleged drug offences in 1989?

18   In 1989, they were fined £82 000 by UEFA following incidents during a 3–1 defeat by Bayern Munich. Bayern

were also fined for their, and their supporters'
behaviour. Who were the Italian team involved?

19 Who was disciplined by his club for being sent off in a
pre-season friendly in the Isle of Wight?

20 What, in their match programme, did Rotherham allege
about the Chesterfield – Fulham match in the 1988
Third Division play-offs?

QUIZ 44

FA CUP 2

1 Which has been the most common result of the FA Cup
final?

2 Who scored in the 1964 final to become the youngest
player to have done so?

3 At which ground, better known for another sport, were
18 of the first 20 finals staged?

4 In which decade did Newcastle last win the FA Cup?

5 Name the two teams who scored three goals in the final
during the 1970s.

6 What was the score of the last all-Merseyside final?

7 What else was notable about Leicester's season when
they reached the final in 1969?

8 Which was the last club to retain the FA Cup?

9 Name either of Chelsea's goalscorers in the 2–2 draw
with Leeds in 1970.

10 Who was the manager when a) Ipswich won the Cup in
1978 and b) West Ham won it in 1964?

11 What role did Major Marindin play in seven successive
finals, 1884–90?

12 Who was the first player to be sent off in an FA Cup
final?

13 Who played in goal for Leeds in the 1965 final?

14 What is the highest number of goals scored by a
defeated team in a final?

15 Name the two teams who have appeared in a record 11 finals.

16 Which, at the time of writing (pre-1989 final) was the last final to go to extra time?

17 When was the last all-London final and who played?

18 Who, in 1971, became the first substitute to score in a final?

19 Name two of the three players to have scored twice in the final in the 1980s.

20 Who were the goalkeepers in the following winning sides – Tottenham 1981, Manchester United 1977, West Ham 1980?

QUIZ 45

SCOTTISH FOOTBALL 2

1 'With a bit of luck in the World Cup I might have been knighted. Instead it looks as if I may be beheaded.' Who said this?

2 From which club did Ian Wallace join Coventry?

3 Which team is known as The Ton?

4 Who was appointed Scotland's first manager in 1954?

5 Which Scottish striker won the PFA's Footballer of the Year and Young Player of the Year in England in 1976?

6 Who captained Aberdeen to the 1970 Cup final win over Celtic – and later led Manchester United to the FA Cup?

7 Who scored 20 league goals for Hearts in 1985–86, a season in which they narrowly failed to win the title?

8 Into which club did Chelsea chairman Ken Bates buy in 1986?

9 What was Scotland's 1986 World Cup group dubbed?

10 . . . In that tournament, whose injury against Denmark prompted him to say, 'The best moment in my career to the worst in 83 minutes'?

11 From which club did Joe Jordan join Leeds?

12 Which club did Ally McLeod leave to manage the national team in 1977?

13 In which year did Ally McCoist make his international debut?

14 What was unusual about the Player of the Year award in 1974?

15 Celtic's 1977 Cup winning team included an English goalkeeper and an Icelander. Name either.

16 Name the six Scottish clubs beginning with the letter A.

17 Which player-coach of Walsall took over the manager's job at Motherwell in 1977–78, and said, on his dismissal in 1978, 'I stood up and was counted'?

18 'We're representing Britain
    We've got to do or die
    England cannae do it
    Cos they didnae qualify'
    Identify the song.

19 Who was the Players' and the Football Writers' Player of the Year in 1988?

20 Identify this club profile: play at Ochilview Park, shirts of maroon with white pin stripes, nickname The Warriors, ground capacity 4000.

QUIZ 46

MIX & MATCH – THE CLASSIFIED

The following sixteen fixtures were played on the first league programme of the year, 2 January 1989. Can you match the jumbled full-time scores and attendances to the games?

FIXTURES	FULL-TIME SCORE
Division One	0–1
Arsenal *v.* Spurs	2–1
Coventry *v.* Sheffield Wednesday	2–0
Luton *v.* Southampton	6–1
Middlesbrough *v.* Manchester United	1–0
Millwall *v.* Charlton	1–2
Newcastle *v.* Derby	0–0
Nottingham Forest *v.* Everton	5–0
QPR *v.* Norwich	1–0
West Ham *v.* Wimbledon	0–1
	2–0
Division Two	3–1
Crystal Palace *v.* Walsall	1–3
Manchester City *v.* Leeds	4–0
WBA *v.* Shrewsbury	1–1
	4–0

Division Three
Bristol City *v.* Bristol Rovers
Sheffield United *v.* Chesterfield
Wolves *v.* Chester

Division Four
Tranmere *v.* Burnley

ATTENDANCE

33 034
24 411
23 191
9 352
45 129
18 346
21 901
7 974
30 055
8 637
26 008
18 411
15 769
12 410
17 025
15 191

PICTURE QUIZ 4

HAIRCUTS

Identify the four players.

1

2

3

4

PICTURE QUIZ 5

BACK TO BACK

Identify the four players with their backs to the camera.

1

2

PICTURE QUIZ 6

OPEN MOUTHED

Identify the three personalities, and the bench, caught with their mouths open.

1

2

3

4

QUIZ 47

NAME THE YEAR

In each question, the events mentioned all happened in the same year. Name the year . . .

1   . . . In which Derby win the Championship, and Leeds are banned from Europe for two seasons.

2   . . . In which Stanley Matthews is knighted and Norman Whiteside is born.

3   . . . In which Charlton play their last match at The Valley, and Peter Reid is Footballer of the Year.

4   . . . In which Czechoslovakia win the European Championships, and Bayern Munich win the European Cup for a third successive time.

5   . . . In which Jeff Astle scores the winning goal in the FA Cup final.

6   . . . In which Wimbledon win the Fourth Division title, and Bob Paisley retires.

7   . . . In which West Germany win the fifth World Cup, and England lose 7–1 to Hungary in Budapest.

8   . . . In which Alf Ramsey is knighted.

9   . . . In which Workington fail to gain re-election, and USSR win the first World Youth Cup.

10   . . . In which West Ham win the FA Cup, and Steve Archibald joins Spurs from Aberdeen.

11   . . . In which the FA celebrates its centenary and Spurs win the Cup Winners Cup.

12   . . . In which the final British Championship match is played, between England and Northern Ireland.

13   . . . In which the League Cup becomes the Milk Cup, and the FA Cup final goes to a replay.

14   . . . In which Swindon beat Arsenal in the League Cup final.

15   . . . In which Russian football reaches the UK through the visit of Moscow Dynamo.

16 . . . In which Leeds beat Juventus in the last Fairs Cup final, and the league title goes to London.

17 . . . In which Uwe Seeler last appears in the World Cup, and Bobby Charlton wins a record 106th cap.

18 . . . In which the League Cup final was last contested between two 'derby' sides.

19 . . . In which England lose their unbeaten home record against Continental opposition.

20 . . . In which Swindon's Chris Kamara becomes the first player to be charged by the police for an incident on the field of play, and John Hollins ceases to be manager of Chelsea.

QUIZ 48

BRITISH FOOTBALL 3

1 Of which club is 1988 Wimbledon champion Stefan Edberg a keen supporter?

2 In which decade did the Pools Panel first sit?

3 Which club did Alf Ramsey manage briefly after England?

4 No southern-based side won the league before 1930. True or false?

5 Which 1988 league match was described by Tom Finney as 'the finest exhibition of football I have ever seen'?

6 In the 1987–88 season, who won the Barclay's Young Eagle of the Year award – Nigel Clough, Paul Gascoigne or Michael Thomas?

7 Manchester United, Real Betis and West Brom are three of Peter Barnes' clubs. Name two of the other three he played for.

8 Of which club is Cliff Bastin the all-time leading goalscorer?

9 Which club, in the days before automatic promotion and relegation, had to seek re-election more than any other?

10 At which University were the laws of football first drafted in 1848 – Durham, Cambridge or Manchester?

11 How many times was the Inverness Thistle *v.* Falkirk Scottish Cup tie postponed in 1978–79 – 5, 9 or 29?

12 Which London club was the first of any First Division club to install floodlights?

13 Why were Reading unable to defend the Simod Cup in 1988–89?

14 Name the only British club to include a 'J' in its name.

15 Which film actor and director was once on the directors' board at Chelsea?

16 Which group of people are responsible for selecting the Barclay's Manager of the Month award?

17 Which entertainer played for Northampton's youth team – Des O'Connor, Val Doonican or Tom Jones?

18 In which year was Peter Shilton born?

19 Which club had their only ever season in Division One in 1974–75?

20 For the 1987–88 season, what was the average number of people arrested in and around football grounds per match in Division One – 5.3, 15.3 or 25.3?

QUIZ 49

THE EIGHTIES

1 Which club was forecasted to be 'the team of the eighties'?

2 Who became Glasgow Rangers' first black player as late as 1988?

3 Name the teams who competed in the first FA Cup final replay to be played at Wembley.

4 Which two Fourth Division clubs attracted a crowd of 80 841 for the 1988 Sherpa Van Trophy final?

5 What two disasters occurred on the last day of the 1985 season?

6 Who scored twice to break the long-running habit of Rush scoring, Liverpool not losing?

7 Which club established 17 club records in winning the 1981 Fourth Division championship?

8 Gary Lineker was the last player to score a hat-trick for England. Who were their opponents?

9 What was the Simod Cup previously called?

10 . . . In which season was it introduced?

11 Which team started 1988 at the top of the Fourth Division and finished it bottom?

12 At the beginning of which season were two substitutes first allowed in the league?

13 Name the two players to have scored own goals in FA Cup finals during the eighties.

14 Which substitute scored in a World Cup final and was then substituted?

15 If, in 1988, Dave Mackay's team played Don Mackay's, which two clubs would be involved?

16 Where did Bradford play their matches at the start of the 1986–87 season?

17 In which year was the last 5–5 draw in the First Division, between QPR and Newcastle?

18 Who won their first Scottish League title in 1983?

19 Which club was prevented from a move to Birmingham when Terry Ramsden bought them out in 1986?

20 Who became the Football League's first sponsors in 1983?

QUIZ 50

SOCCER & TV

1 In which decade did *Match of the Day* appear?

2 What team does TV's Stavros support?

3 What was the subject of the BBC drama *Playing For Real*?

4 . . . And which talented soccer journalist wrote the screenplay?

5 Which impressionist is an Honorary Vice President of Stockport County?

6 Which club banned television cameras and planned to set up their own film unit?

7 Name either of the teams involved in the first Sunday league fixture to be televised live?

8 Which footballer presenter had a spell managing Portsmouth?

9 The Mercantile Credit Classic, to celebrate the league's Centenary, was the most televised football match ever shown. True or false?

10 Which TV series did Terry Venables co-write?

11 Which nation's goal against England prompted the commentator to invoke the names of Margaret Thatcher, Princess Diana and Sir Winston Churchill?

12 In which decade was the first FA Cup final to be shown (partially) on television?

13 To the nearest 10%, what was the estimated percentage of Denmark's entire adult population who watched their games in the 1986 World Cup?

14 . . . During that World Cup, whose role on the ITV panel prompted the *Observer* to write, 'His only plausible function is to make Kevin Keegan look like an intellectual'?

15 Of which club is Emlyn Hughes a director?

16 Why was the screening of the 1968 FA Cup final between Everton and WBA a television milestone in football?

17 Which former player and manager appeared in the television drama, *Those Glory Glory Days*?

18 Which club was the subject of an investigation by *World in Action*?

19 Of which club is golf commentator Peter Alliss a lifelong follower?

20 What was the name of the former TV quiz game, based around a football pitch, in which contestants might take Route One to goal?

QUIZ 51

LEFT BACKS

1 In the Leeds FA Cup final teams of 1970, 1972 and 1973, three different players wore the No. 3 shirt. Name them.

2 Who is the most expensive left back in British transfer history?

3 Which left back missed a penalty in the 1988 Littlewoods Cup final?

4 Name the former Stoke and England left back of the 1970s who in 1989 was coaching the youth team at Port Vale.

5 Who was the last Manchester United player to wear the Scotland No. 3 shirt?

6 Which left back, with over 400 club appearances, won an FA Cup winners medal in 1975?

7 Who is the Chelsea defender who has held three different passports at once – Australian, Italian and British?

8 Who typically partnered Pat Rice on the other flank at club level?

9 In the 1987–88 season, four players wore the No. 3 shirt for Manchester United. Name them.

10 Who was the West German left back in the 1986 World Cup final?

11 Which Chelsea left back of the 1970s later went on to manage them?

12 Who was the left back who scored in the 1974 FA Cup final?

13 He played for Portsmouth, Ipswich and Southampton, and later became a manager. Who is he?

14 Which of the following is a left back – Ian Evans, Ian Dawes or Ian Morgan?

15 His brother is a contemporary manager, he played left back for Scotland in the early 1980s. Who is he?

16 Who was England's left back in the World Cup winning team?

17 Which former left back became manager of Exeter in 1988 after being dismissed by Bristol City?

18 A Merseyside based Welsh international born in Belgium . . .

19 Who was the Arsenal left back who started his first full international in 1968, with Keith Newton at right back?

20 No left back has ever scored in a World Cup final. True or false?

QUIZ 52

EUROPEAN & INTERNATIONAL 3

1 Which club side play at the Nou Camp?

2 Peter Osgood won less than 10 caps for England. True or false?

3 Apart from Torino, what is Turin's other famous club side?

4 Since the war, only three players with the surname beginning with V have played for England. Name two of them.

5 Who won the league title in Italy in 1987–88 season?

6 . . . Who was the top scorer in the German league that year?

7 Which Soviet player was 1986 European Footballer of the Year?

8 Name three of the fluid French midfield who led them to the European Championships.

9 Only two teams failed to gain a point in the 1988 European Championships. One was England – who was the other?

10 Before Ian Rush, who was the most expensive Briton to join an Italian club?

11 Only four clubs won the West German league during the 1970s – name three of them.

12 Who was the South American Footballer of the Year who starred for Colombia in the 1988 friendly at Wembley?

13 How many members does FIFA have – 50, 100 or 150?

14 Name the two Bayern Munich players who have won the title of European Footballer of the Year.

15 In which country do club side AEK play?

16 Which British club is second to Liverpool in terms of most European club trophies?

17 Complete the following North American soccer club names: . . . . Whitecaps, Chicago . . . . , New York . . . .

18 In which cities do Internazionale and Lazio play?

19 Who were the last team to retain the European Cup?

20 Complete the following club names – AS . . . ., CSKA . . . ., Odense . . . ., ... Liege.

QUIZ 53

PUB GAMES

1 Name the five English league clubs whose full names both begin and end with the same letter.

2 Name the 16 goalkeepers to have played for England since the beginning of 1960.

3 Name the eight managers of Leeds since Don Revie.

4 Name the last ten goalscorers in FA Cup finals to have finished 1–0.

5 In 1947–48, there were nine Lancashire teams in Division One. Name them.

6 Name the ten players to have been voted the Football Writers Footballer of the Year in the period 1970–79.

7 Name the seven British clubs whose full names include three or more words.

8 Name the 16 clubs in the Italian First Division in the season 1987–88.

9 Name the six Scottish internationals of the 1980s whose forename and surname both begin with the same letter.

10   Name the six Scottish clubs whose full names both begin and end with the same letter.

11   There are 26 English clubs whose full names comprise only one word. Name them.

QUIZ 54

1989

1   Who led the First, Second, Third and Fourth Divisions on January 1st?

2   Which former FA Cup final scorer played his first Division One match for eight years in January and duly scored for Norwich?

3   Which was the only minor league club to beat First Division opposition in the FA Cup?

4   Which Scottish manager, previously of Rangers and Seville, took over at bottom of the league Colchester?

5   Who became the first club ever to sign a Soviet player?

6   Who displaced Ron Atkinson in Spain?

7   Who scored four goals for Forest in their 5–2 victory over QPR in the Littlewoods Cup quarter-final?

8   Why did Carlisle, nearing the bottom of the Fourth Division, attract a crowd of over 10 000 for their first league game of the year?

9   Which Manchester United player was described by *The Guardian* as 'the bargain of the season – for Bristol City who sold him'?

10   Which was the last North Eastern club left in the FA Cup?

11   What was the incident comically described as 'A clear case of the shit hitting the fan'?

12   Early in the year, a season ticket holder at a First Division club reported that club to the trading standards officer for an alleged breach of the Trades Description Act, feeling their performances couldn't be described as football. Which club?

13 Five players of the 200 Club of first class goals were still present in the league. Name three of them.

14 Which manager described his team as 'the most brainless in the world' after their 3–3 draw with Colchester in the FA Cup?

15 For how much was Peter Reid transferred to QPR from Everton?

16 What was the nationality of Milos Drizic who was refused a work permit allowing him to play for Southampton?

17 Who retired as Secretary of the FA after 16 years in office?

18 Which 34 year old headbutted a spectator after being sent off for the first time in his career and was subsequently charged with assault?

19 Against whom was England's first international of the year?

20 Which was the last Fourth Division club left in the FA Cup?

QUIZ 55

TRANSFERS 2

1 Who was the first million pound footballer?

2 Who was the first British player to be transferred for £100 000?

3 Who, in 1979, was transferred for £516 000 from Middlesbrough to West Brom, a record fee between British clubs?

4 From which club did Perry Groves join Arsenal?

5 From which French club did Ray Wilkins join Rangers?

6 What was the length of time between the first £½ million and the first £1 million transfers in Britain – five weeks, five months or 15 months?

7 In which year did Kevin Keegan join Hamburg and Kenny Dalglish join Liverpool?

8   Who was the first British player to be transferred for £1 million on *two* occasions?

9   Who joined Newcastle from Palmeiras in August 1987?

10 Who were the first brothers to be involved in an exchange transfer, between QPR and Sheffield Wednesday?

11 Who, when released by Real Madrid in 1984, became the first £1 million player to be given a free transfer?

12 From which club did John Toshack join Liverpool in November 1970?

13 Who, in June 1957, became the first British player to be transferred overseas?

14 Who did Celtic buy from Motherwell having sold Brian McClair to Manchester United?

15 For which Oxford player did Inter Milan bid £1.3 million in August 1987?

16 Who created a record transfer fee between England and Scotland when he was transferred for £1.5 million?

17 Which left winger created club records both for transfer fee paid and received for Burnley?

18 From which club was Adrian Heath transferred to Everton for £700 000 in 1982?

19 From whom did West Ham sign Liam Brady at a bargain £100 000?

20 Who, in June 1988, became Britain's most expensive goalkeeper?

QUIZ 56

BACK PAGE

1   'SPURS SCOOP THE WORLD'. Who were the players involved in this 1978 story?

2   Which QPR player confessed 'YES, I TAKE DRUGS' in 1978?

3   'THE ANIMALS ARE COMING'. In which year did this headline appear and why?

4   'SHANKLY IS DEAD'. What was the year of the great man's death?

5   'QUEEN IN BRAWL AT PALACE' said *The Guardian*. Who was the 'Queen' referred to?

6   'THE MAN WHO WANTS TO BE MR UNITED'. To whom was the *Daily Mirror* referring in February 1984?

7   'THE FINAL SHAME'. To which 1980s event was this headline referring?

8   'I'LL SIGN . . . .'. What was the Rangers manager Graeme Souness' vow in 1986?

9   Why did the *Sun* headline of 23 June 1986 say 'OUTCHA'?

10   To whom did Everton chairman Philip Carter tell 'STAY AWAY YOU SCUM' in 1987?

11   In which year was it considered 'TIME IS RUNNING OUT FOR WOLVES' by *The Guardian*?

12   Which event in 1981 did the *Daily Star* consider 'PERHAPS THE MOST IMPORTANT MILESTONE THIS CENTURY'?

13   'SOCCER BOSS IN PROBE'. Who was the Manchester United chairman accused such by the *Daily Express* in 1980?

14   'HOW I MADE KEVIN INTO A SAINT'. Who was the manager and the player involved in this story?

15   'REVIE QUITS OVER AGGRO'. In which year did Revie give up the England job?

16   From which club did 'CLUB WIVES OUST DOC' in 1977?

17   Why did the *Daily Express* refer to 'LAW'S LAST SAD WORD' in 1974?

18   'NOW US BEATS US AT SOCCER' said a tired *Daily Express* headline. In which year?

19   Which tournament brought out the following *Sun* headlines – 'YOU LUCKY LOT', 'YOU MUGS', 'BELT UP YOU BIG MOUTHS' and 'LIARS AND CHEATS'?

20   Who claimed in a 1989 headline, 'I'M NOT GOING TO CRACK UP LIKE BESTIE'?

PICTURE QUIZ 7

ALL IN THE GAME

1 What was the outcome of this incident?

2 In which decade was this photograph of Renton FC taken?

3 Name the two players in this on the ball incident.

4 Who is this
club chairman?

PICTURE QUIZ 8

FLOWER OF YOUTH

Identify the four personalities.

1

2

3

4

PICTURE QUIZ 9

LEFT HALVES

Identify the three players.

1

2

3

PICTURE QUIZ 10

BEHIND THE BALL

Identify the three players.

1

QUIZ 57

THAT'S FOOTBALL, BRIAN

A mixed bag of questions with no particular theme.

1   What is the West German league officially known as?

2   Who won the Youth Cup in 1988?

3   What is the international company behind Juventus, and what is their chairman's name?

4   George Best was never voted European Footballer of the Year. True or false?

5   In 1984, which Ipswich player, at 16 years 57 days, became the youngest player to score in a First Division match?

6   Name the four league clubs whose name begins with the letters Ch.

7   After which former player have Newcastle named their new stand?

8   Who preceded Ron Atkinson as manager of Manchester United?

9   No Fourth Division side has ever reached the final of the League Cup. True or false?

10   Which club might make the substitution Dennis for Law?

11   In 1923 Wembley staged its first FA Cup final. What Wembley first was staged in 1924?

12   Which First Division side had the lowest average home attendance for the 1987–88 season?

13   . . . Who had the highest Second Division average?

14   . . . Sunderland easily led the Third; who was next?

15   What is the name of the famous park that separates Anfield and Goodison Park?

16   Where did Wimbledon finish in their first season in the First Division in 1987?

17   How many Charity Shields did Liverpool contest in 14 seasons to 1987?

18 Which 1986 World Cup referee is headmaster of a primary school in Co. Durham?

19 When Dixie Dean scored 60 goals in 39 matches for Everton, how many were with his head – 5, 20 or 38?

20 Who were England's opponents in the match dubbed 'High Noon' in Mexico?

QUIZ 58

92 UP

Each club in the Football League (up to end of 1989 season) has a question related to it.

1 **ALDERSHOT** Never been out of Division Three or Four. True or false?

2 **ARSENAL** Who was Arsenal's Player of the Year for 1988?

3 **ASTON VILLA** To whom did Villa lose in the 1982 World Club Championship?

4 **BARNSLEY** Name either of the two members of the early 1970s Leeds side that have since managed Barnsley.

5 **BIRMINGHAM** Which club did Birmingham beat 9–1 in a Division Two game in 1954?

6 **BLACKBURN** Who was the Blackburn manager immediately before Bobby Saxton?

7 **BLACKPOOL** When were Blackpool last in Division One – 1969, 1971 or 1975?

8 **BOLTON** Which former Bolton star is now the club president?

9 **BOURNEMOUTH** What was the score in Bournemouth's record victory in which Ted MacDougall personally scored nine?

10 **BRADFORD** Which former Derby and England centre back had a spell as manager?

11 **BRENTFORD** What is the name of Brentford's ground?

12 **BRIGHTON** Who is the most expensive player to be sold by Brighton, for £900 000 in 1981?

13 **BRISTOL CITY** What trophy did City win in 1985–86?

14 **BRISTOL ROVERS** Whose ground have Rovers shared having moved from Eastville?

15 **BURNLEY** In which two European competitions have Burnley played?

16 **BURY** Which First Division scalp did Bury claim in the 1988 Littlewoods Cup?

17 **CAMBRIDGE** Who, between 1975–80, notched up a record number of league goals for the club?

18 **CARDIFF** To the nearest 10 000, what is Ninian Park's capacity?

19 **CARLISLE** For whom did Vancouver Whitecaps pay £275 000 in 1986?

20 **CHARLTON** Who was the Danish international who played for Charlton in the early 1980s?

21 **CHELSEA** Which full back made a record number of league appearances for the club?

22 **CHESTER** Which centre forward left the club for £300 000 in 1980?

23 **CHESTERFIELD** The club has never been in Division One. True or false?

24 **COLCHESTER** Colchester had their best run in the FA Cup in 1970–71. Which round did they reach?

25 **COVENTRY** Whom did Coventry sell to Forest for £1 250 000?

26 **CREWE** Which First Division club did Crewe lead 2–0 in the FA Cup in 1989, before losing 3–2?

27 **CRYSTAL PALACE** Who made 571 league appearances for Palace, 1973–88?

28 **DARLINGTON** Which former player has since played for Scotland and captained Coventry?

29 **DERBY** Which centre forward joined Derby via Arsenal, Manchester United and Ajax?

30 **DONCASTER** Where do Doncaster play their home games?

31 **EVERTON** Name two of the three managers before Colin Harvey.

32 **EXETER** What colour shirts do Exeter play in at home?

33 **FULHAM** Who managed Fulham before Ray Lewington, and now manages a First Division club?

34 **GILLINGHAM** By what score did Gillingham beat Chesterfield in September 1987 to create a club record?

35 **GRIMSBY** Which man, later legend, was Grimsby's second manager after the war?

36 **HALIFAX** Halifax have never had an internationally capped player. True or false?

37 **HARTLEPOOL** Which top manager began his managerial career here?

38 **HEREFORD** Which Hereford player scored a BBC Goal of the Season?

39 **HUDDERSFIELD** Which player did Town sell to Manchester City for a club record fee in 1985?

40 **HULL** Which former Arsenal manager was the club's most capped player – for Northern Ireland?

41 **IPSWICH** Name the two Ipswich managers who have gone on to manage England.

42 **LEEDS** Which winger played for Leeds between 1965 and 1979 and then 1983–86?

43 **LEICESTER** In which season were Leicester last in Division One?

44 **LEYTON ORIENT** They have never been in the First Division. True or false?

45 **LINCOLN** Who led Lincoln to their last Fourth Division championship?

46 **LIVERPOOL** Which No. 11 made a record 640 club appearances?

47 **LUTON** Which Luton defender is also one of the club's coaches?

48 **MAN CITY** After which former player is a football fanzine named?

49 **MAN UNITED** When did United last win the league?

50 **MANSFIELD** Which current national manager previously managed Mansfield?

51 **MIDDLESBROUGH** Who is Bruce Rioch's assistant, a former Derby colleague?

52 **MILLWALL** Which central defender made a record 523 appearances for the club, 1967–82?

53 **NEWCASTLE** Who is Newcastle's all-time top scorer for the club?

54 **NORTHAMPTON** Which former Villa manager is now in charge at the County Ground?

55 **NORWICH** Name two of the three players to be transferred for £1 million from Norwich.

56 **NOTTINGHAM FOREST** Forest have won the league just once. True or false?

57 **NOTTS COUNTY** Who was the former Liverpool centre back who went on to manage County?

58 **OLDHAM** What is the name of Oldham's ground?

59 **OXFORD** Which Oxford player of recent seasons has the unusual distinction of a double-barrelled name?

60 **PETERBOROUGH** Which is the highest division Peterborough have played in?

61 **PLYMOUTH** Which politician is a well known Plymouth supporter?

62 **PORTSMOUTH** For whom did Portsmouth receive £915 000 in 1984?

63 **PORT VALE** What was Port Vale's giant-killing act in the 1988 FA Cup?

64 **PRESTON** Preston's record receipts were v. Burnley in April 1988 – in what competition?

65 **QPR** What is the highest position achieved in the league by Rangers?

66 **READING** Which trophy did Reading win in 1988?

67 **ROCHDALE** Name Rochdale's ground.

68 **ROTHERHAM** Who was the keeper for whom Everton paid £180 000 in 1985?

69 **SCARBOROUGH** Against whom did Scarborough play their first game in Division Four?

70 **SCUNTHORPE** Which player with 63 England caps began his career here?

71 **SHEFFIELD UNITED** Which former England star was manager before Ian Porterfield?

72 **SHEFFIELD WEDNESDAY** Which England goalkeeper is the club's most capped player?

73 **SHREWSBURY** Which trophy did Shrewsbury win in 1977, 1979, 1984 and 1985?

74 **SOUTHAMPTON** From where does striker Matthew Le Tissier hail?

75 **SOUTHEND** Who is the former club manager with an OBE to his name?

76 **STOCKPORT** Name the former Manchester City right winger of the 1970s who went on to manage Stockport.

77 **STOKE** How many league clubs were founded before Stoke?

78 **SUNDERLAND** Which keeper made a record 537 appearances for the club?

79 **SWANSEA** How many seasons did Swansea play in the First Division at the start of the 1980s?

80 **SWINDON** Who scored twice in Swindon's famous League Cup final win over Arsenal?

81 **TORQUAY** Which ex-Manchester United manager had three spells in charge of Torquay?

82 **TOTTENHAM** When did Spurs last win the championship?

83 **TRANMERE** In 1935, Tranmere won a trophy you wouldn't expect them to have played in. Which?

84 **WALSALL** Which forward did Walsall sell to Birmingham in 1978 and buy back in 1979?

85 **WATFORD** Watford have never played in Europe. True or false?

86 **WEST BROMWICH ALBION** Which World Cup winners medal holder is a former manager at The Hawthorns?

87 **WEST HAM** West Ham have only played in one European competition, the Cup Winners Cup. True or false?

88 **WIGAN** Which trophy did Wigan win in 1985?

89 **WIMBLEDON** How many seasons have Wimbledon played in Division Two in their club history?

90 **WOLVES** From which club did Steve Bull join Wolves?

91 **WREXHAM** Which keeper was Wrexham's most capped player?

92 **YORK** Against which club did York gain record receipts in an FA Cup Fifth Round tie in 1986?

ANSWERS

QUIZ 1

A – Z 1

A   Aldridge (John)

B   Blissett (Luther)

C   Camacho

D   Dibble

E   Everton

F   Forfar Athletic

G   Grimsby Town

H   Hughes (Emlyn)

I   Iran

J   Juventus

K   Krankl (Hans)

L   Luton Town

M   Masson (Don)

N   Nottingham Forest

O   Osborne (Roger)

P   Pickles

Q   Quinn (Jimmy)

R   Riva

S   Stockport County

T   Tunisia

U   Ujpest

V   Victoria Ground (Stoke)

W   Watson (Dave)

X   Xuereb (Daniel)

Y   Yorath (Terry)

Z   Zondervan (Romeo)

QUIZ 2

EUROPEAN &
INTERNATIONAL 1

1   Kevin Keegan (1979)

2   Karl-Heinz
    Rummenigge (Bayern
    Munich to Internazionale,
    1984, £3 million)

3   True (four semi-finals,
    once winners)

4   Peter Lorimer

5   Zico

6   Morten Olsen

7   South America

8   Preston North End

9   Santos

10   Tarantini

11   Real Sociedad

12   Rumania

13   Brazilian

14   Falcao

15   Uruguay

16   Seven

17   Greece

18   FC Magdeburg

19   Benfica, Sporting
     Lisbon, FC Porto

20   Argentina

QUIZ 3

MANAGERS 1

1   Brian Clough

2   Harry Catterick

3   Willie Ormond

4   Ipswich

5   Steve Coppell

6   Allan Brown

7   Helmut Schoen

8   Billy Bremner (they had
    their first win in six
    games)

9   True

10   Alan Durban

11   Brian Clough

12   Graham Taylor

13   John Sillett

14   Dave Mackay (1975)

15   Crewe Alexandra

16   Tony Barton

17   Ted Drake

18   Terry Venables

19   George Graham

20   QPR, Oxford Utd

ANSWERS

QUIZ 4

BRITISH FOOTBALL 1

1 Everton (all but four since their foundation in 1888)
2 Preston
3 1980s (1989 – Arsenal)
4 Dumbarton
5 29
6 Jimmy McGrory
7 Swansea
8 Liverpool; 6th
9 1958
10 Huddersfield
11 York City (101)
12 Billy McNeill
13 Tottenham
14 Oxford United
15 Bristol City
16 True
17 Jackie Charlton (629)
18 Scarborough
19 True
20 QPR

QUIZ 5

QUOTES

1 Malcolm Macdonald
2 Bobby Robson
3 Jan Molby
4 Australia's
5 Joe Mercer
6 Sammy Lee
7 Howard Kendall
8 Bobby Moore on his arrest in Colombia in 1970
9 Wimbledon
10 Alex Ferguson

11 Paul Power
12 Asa Hartford
13 Paul Gascoigne
14 Brian Clough, on his consideration for the Wales job part-time
15 Bob Paisley

QUIZ 6

THE SIXTIES

1 Oxford United
2 Denis Law
3 Ray Wilson
4 Burnley
5 Five
6 1961
7 Twice
8 9–3
9 Dunfermline
10 Gilmar
11 The League Cup
12 USSR
13 Pietro Anastasi
14 Sir Stanley Rous
15 Peru and Argentina
16 Matt Busby, Bill Nicholson
17 Chile
18 Arthur Rowley
19 The Sixth
20 Injury – the law was amended the following year to allow them for any reason

ANSWERS

QUIZ 7

FA CUP 1

1 1971

2 Nat Lofthouse controversially barged Harry Gregg over the line to win the final

3 *Abide With Me*

4 Allan Clarke

5 Arsenal (5.45)

6 Walthamstow Avenue

7 Trevor Bailey

8 Ossie Ardiles (The Falklands)

9 Bolton Wanderers

10 Newcastle United

11 Walsall

12 West Ham (1980)

13 Bert Trautmann

14 Howard Kendall (17 yr 345 days)

15 True

16 Southampton (1976)

17 Tommy Docherty

18 Roy Dwight

19 Frank Stapleton (Arsenal 1979, Man Utd 1983)

20 Brighton

QUIZ 8

MILESTONES

1 1981–82

2 Liverpool

3 5–4

4 1950s (1956)

5 1976

6 Tottenham (Cup Winners Cup, 1963)

7 Jimmy Dickinson

8 Kenny Dalglish

9 1986

10 Preston North End (1888–89)

11 1973

12 1920s (1929)

13 Leeds United (1968)

14 1960–61

15 1930s (1933)

16 Freight Rover

17 1905

18 Keith Peacock

19 1974

20 Aberdeen

ANSWERS

QUIZ 9

MILLION POUNDERS

£6 900 000	Diego Maradona	Barcelona – Napoli, 1984
£5 500 000	Ruud Gullit	PSV Eindhoven – AC Milan, 1987
£4 800 000	Diego Maradona	Argentinos Juniors – Barcelona, 1982
£3 200 000	Ian Rush	Liverpool – Juventus, 1987
£2 750 000	Gary Lineker	Everton – Barcelona, 1986
£2 300 000	Mark Hughes	Man Utd – Barcelona, 1986
£1 900 000	Peter Beardsley	Newcastle – Liverpool, 1987
£1 500 000	Bryan Robson	WBA – Man Utd, 1981
£1 500 000	Ray Wilkins	Man Utd – AC Milan, 1984
£1 500 000	Richard Gough	Spurs – Rangers, 1987
£1 469 000	Andy Gray	Aston Villa – Wolves, 1979
£1 437 000	Steve Daley	Wolves – Man City, 1979
£1 350 000	Kenny Sansom	Crystal Palace – Arsenal, 1980
£1 250 000	Kevin Reeves	Norwich – Man City, 1980
£1 250 000	Ian Wallace	Coventry – Notts Forest, 1980
£1 250 000	Clive Allen	Arsenal – Crystal Palace, 1980
£1 250 000	Garry Birtles	Notts Forest – Man Utd, 1980
£1 180 000	Trevor Francis	Birmingham – Notts Forest, 1979
£1 000 000	Justin Fashanu	Norwich – Notts Forest, 1981
£1 000 000	Ian Ferguson	St Mirren – Rangers, 1988

QUIZ 10

WORLD CUP 1

1   Brazil

2   Mexico (1970, 1986)

3   Viv Richards

4   Cesar Luis Menotti

5   Haiti

6   Antonio Cabrini

7   Uruguay

8   Italy (1938)

9   Vava

10   France and West Germany

11   1950

12   1970

13   USSR

14   1954

15   Uwe Seeler's

16   Gerry Armstrong

17   Algeria

18   Socrates

19   Bulldog Bobby

20   None of them

ANSWERS

QUIZ 11

WHO'S WHO 1

1 Laurie Cunningham
2 Kevin Keegan
3 Tony Dorigo
4 Kenny Dalglish
5 Gerry Daly
6 Derek Fazackerley
7 Just Fontaine
8 Gerd Muller
9 Ray Clemence
10 Dundee United
11 Brian Clough
12 Rachid Harkouk
13 Mick Harford
14 Peter Beardsley
15 Pat Jennings
16 Danny McGrain
17 Dixie Dean
18 Stanley Matthews
19 Graeme Souness
20 Nigel Spackman

QUIZ 12

FORWARD THINKING

1 Phil Boyer
2 Marco van Basten
3 John Wark
4 Ten (for Luton v. Bristol Rovers, 1936)
5 Fastest own goal
6 Jimmy Greaves (220)
7 Gerd Muller
8 Ian Rush (1984)
9 Jairzinho
10 Kenny Dalglish
11 Bob Latchford (1977–78)

12 Peter Withe (20)
13 Ted MacDougall
14 Ruud Gullit and Marco van Basten
15 AC Milan, Verona
16 Clive Allen
17 Malcolm Macdonald (v. Cyprus, 1975)
18 Len Shackleton
19 Frank McAvennie
20 Allan Clarke, Ian Porterfield, Bobby Stokes, Roger Osborne

QUIZ 13

OUTSIDE THE BOX

1 Tony Pass
2 True (19 272)
3 False (10 555)
4 Phil Neal
5 Dundee United
6 Terry Butcher
7 Scotland
8 Manchester City
9 Brian McClair's
10 Spurs and Wolves (UEFA Cup 1972)
11 Aston Villa (1896–97)
12 Nottingham Forest (1978)
13 The Duke of Kent
14 Colombia
15 Northern Ireland
16 Luton (beat Arsenal 3–2)
17 European Nations Cup
18 Scotland
19 Darlington, Derby, Doncaster
20 Wembley

ANSWERS

QUIZ 14

SCOTTISH FOOTBALL 1

1 Tommy Walker
2 B. A. Robertson
3 Fine Fare
4 1975
5 First to be decided on penalties
6 James Farry
7 Queen's Park
8 Clyde
9 Willie Miller
10 Woods, Roberts, McAvennie, Butcher
11 Gemmell, Chalmers
12 Hearts
13 Aberdeen (1983)
14 Danny McGrain
15 Liverpool (though he never played for the first team)
16 Third Lanark
17 Rangers (1873) to Celtic's 1888
18 Seville
19 Joe Harper
20 Hibernian

QUIZ 15

BEAT THE INTRO 1

1 Eusebio
2 Norwich City
3 Johnny Haynes
4 Mirandinha
5 Denis Law
6 Ruud Gullit
7 Billy Meredith
8 Hartlepool
9 Lawrie Sanchez
10 Joe Royle

QUIZ 16

MORE QUOTES

1 'Liverpool and Liverpool Reserves'
2 Duncan McKenzie
3 Whymark wasn't playing
4 Wolves
5 'Brazilian' (said Pele at the 1986 World Cup)
6 1980 FA Cup final, West Ham *v.* Arsenal
7 Brian Clough
8 Liverpool (by Bob Paisley)
9 Watford
10 'Ossie's going to Wembley'
11 Jasper Carrott
12 Football directors
13 Tommy Docherty
14 Jimmy Melia
15 Billy Bremner
16 Brian Clough
17 Charlie Nicholas
18 Newcastle
19 Bill Shankly
20 *Auf Wiedersehen, Pet*

ANSWERS

QUIZ 17

SING WHEN YOU'RE WINNING

1 'Back Home' by the England World Cup Squad

2 Rod Stewart

3 The Valley

4 'London 0 Hull 4'

5 'The Worst Song Ever'

6 'This Time'

7 Leyton Orient

8 Cyril Knowles (as in 'Nice One Cyril')

9 Peters and Lee

10 'All I want for Christmas is a Dukla Prague away kit'

11 Richard Jobson

12 George Best

13 Gordon John Sinclair

14 Terry Venables

15 Liverpool

16 'Cinnamon Stick' (make a point of hearing it if you can)

17 Number 5

18 Paper Lace

19 'Diamond Lights'

20 Craig Johnston

8 Steve Norris (Telford), Phil Derbyshire (Stafford), Paul Davies (Kidderminster)

9 Barnet

10 Barnet

11 Tooting & Mitcham

12 Chorley

13 Croydon, Carshalton, Sutton United

14 The Football Combination

15 Middlesbrough

16 Edgware Town

17 Steve Butler (Maidstone)

18 Wales (2–0)

19 Scarborough

20 Merthyr Tydfil

QUIZ 18

MINOR LEAGUE

1 Above

2 Kidderminster Harriers

3 Enfield

4 Workington

5 Vauxhall-Opel

6 Yeovil Town

7 Barrie Williams

ANSWERS

QUIZ 19

CAPTAINS

1 1980
2 Daniel Passarella
3 Phil Neale
4 Carlos Alberto
5 Dave Beasant (1988)
6 John Greig
7 Aston Villa
8 Anton Rattin
9 Brian Labone
10 Ronald Koeman
11 David Nish
12 Norwich, Man City, QPR
13 Dennis Mortimer
14 Steve Perryman
15 George Foster
16 Dennis Waterman
17 Socrates
18 Alan Hansen
19 Billy Wright
20 Dino Zoff

QUIZ 20

GEOGRAPHY TEST 1

1 F (Reading)
2 L (Spurs)
3 C (Edinburgh)
4 A (Chester-le-Street)
5 B (Northampton)
6 E (Nottingham Forest)
7 I (Shrewsbury)
8 J (Wolves)
9 G (Carlisle)
10 D (Glasgow)
11 K (Liverpool)
12 H (Plymouth)

QUIZ 21

RAPID FIRE

1 Gillingham
2 Italy
3 George Curtis
4 Ron Greenwood
5 Blackpool
6 Joey Jones
7 Alex Ferguson
8 1958
9 Atletico Bilbao
10 44
11 Bobby Moore
12 Don Howe
13 Gigg Lane
14 Ted Drake
15 Cambridge United
16 Chris Woods
17 17
18 Peter Shilton
19 False (once, in 1986)
20 Second (one season)

QUIZ 22

RECORD BREAKERS

1 Nine
2 909
3 Notts County
4 A hat-trick
5 Liam Brady
6 Nottingham Forest
7 Wrexham
8 135 826
9 Ten
10 19
11 Jimmy Greaves (six for Chelsea, 1960–61)
12 Ferenc Puskas
13 Leslie Compton

ANSWERS

14 They didn't concede a goal

15 Rivelino

16 Sheffield

17 Pat Jennings (119)

18 Bob Paisley

19 Sixth Round

20 England

QUIZ 23

GROUNDS

1 Old Trafford

2 Turf Moor (Burnley's)

3 The Recreation Ground

4 Bucharest

5 West Ham – The Boleyn Ground

6 Played in England – at Anfield

7 Brentford's

8 Benfica

9 Walsall

10 Anfield

11 Loftus Road, Stamford Bridge and Craven Cottage

12 Ibrox

13 Millwall

14 White Hart Lane (Spurs)

15 Football Grounds Improvement Trust

16 Burnden Park (Bolton)

17 Carlisle and Darlington

18 Sunderland (Roker Park)

19 Sheffield Wednesday

20 Bramall Lane (Sheffield United)

QUIZ 24

HAPPY FAMILIES

1 The Futcher twins, Paul and Ron

2 The Allens

3 Zico

4 Ken and Terry Hibbitt

5 The first club to field three brothers in the same side, the Wallaces

6 The Robledo brothers

7 Clarke

8 Sunderland

9 Goalkeeper

10 Tommy Docherty's son Michael

11 Charlton family, through Bobby and Jack

12 The Comptons

13 John Bond (son Kevin) and Ken Brown (son Kenny)

14 Steve Gatting

15 Charles

16 Milburn

17 Tony and Mark Hateley

18 The Sealeys

19 Brentford

20 Nigel Clough

ANSWERS

QUIZ 25

TEAM SHEETS

1 Pat Crerand, John Aston

2 Tostao, Rivelino

3 Dave Watson, Dennis Tueart

4 George Cohen, Alan Ball

5 Steve Archibald, Glenn Hoddle

6 Jim Leighton, Graeme Souness

7 Phil Thompson, Paul Mariner

8 Frank McLintock, George Graham

9 Sepp Maier, Wolfgang Overath

10 David Nish, Mike Pejic

QUIZ 26

BEFORE & AFTER

	PREDECESSOR	SUCCESSOR
1	Leeds United	Chelsea
2	Brian Clough	Jock Stein
3	Dundee United	Aberdeen
4	Hungary	Czechoslovakia
5	Bobby Charlton	George Best
6	Czechoslovakia	France
7	Derby County	Leeds United
8	Kerry Dixon	Clive Allen
9	Lincoln City	Luton Town
10	Norwich City	Millwall

ANSWERS

QUIZ 27

SOCCER & POLITICS

1 Ruud Gullit

2 Kevin Keegan

3 Robert Maxwell

4 Harold Wilson

5 Jimmy Hill

6 Justice Popplewell

7 Henry Kissinger

8 The name Jimmy Carter

9 Hartlepool

10 The PFA (Professional Footballers' Association)

11 Roy Hattersley

12 Four

13 Dennis Howell

14 Harold Wilson

15 Richard Crossman

16 Football Spectators Bill

17 1954

18 Joao Havelange

19 David Evans

20 South Africa

QUIZ 28

THE SEVENTIES

1 Viv Anderson

2 One (Chelsea – Leeds)

3 Meadowbank Thistle

4 One (Derby County)

5 1974

6 Wimbledon

7 Manchester City

8 Wolves and Liverpool (Liverpool's 3–1 win gave them the title and sealed Wolves' relegation)

9 False (Arsenal, 1971)

10 Tostao (1971), Pele (1973), Zico (1977)

11 Teofillo Cubillas (1972), Mario Kempes (1978)

12 Glasgow Rangers

13 Bill McGarry

14 1974

15 Peter Ward

16 Crystal Palace

17 York, Bournemouth, Norwich, Southampton

18 Aston Villa

19 Cambridge United

20 Chelsea's

QUIZ 29

BRITISH FOOTBALL 2

1 True

2 Peter Knowles

3 John Barnes

4 Leicester, Man City

5 Newport County

6 Reading, Rochdale, Rotherham

7 Scunthorpe

8 Crystal Palace *v.* Brighton

9 Jack Dunnett

10 Stanley Matthews

11 None (Chelsea, Sheffield United, Rotherham)

12 Manchester United

13 Paul Gascoigne

14 Sunderland

15 West Ham (as in 'Come on you Irons')

16 Southport

17 Kevin Keegan

18 Watford

19 John Aldridge

20 Martin Bone

ANSWERS

QUIZ 30

A – Z 2

A   Accrington

B   Blanchflower (Danny)

C   Chile

D   Dumbarton

E   Eastville

F   Feyenoord

G   Glentoran

H   Hadjuk

I   Ince (Paul)

J   Jules Rimet

K   Kilmarnock

L   Lineker (Gary)

M   Millwall

N   Neeskens (Johann)

O   Oxford

P   Pele

Q   QPR

R   Rensenbrink (Robbie)

S   Stoke City

T   Torquay United

U   USA

V   Vetch Field

W   Walsall

X   Crewe Alexandra

Y   Yeats (Ron)

Z   Zico

QUIZ 31

MANAGERS 2

1. Millwall
2. Altrincham
3. Seven
4. Dave Bassett
5. Malcolm Allison
6. Martin Dobson, Frank Casper

7. Bristol Rovers
8. Mark Lawrenson (Liverpool player earlier in the season)
9. Steve Perryman
10. Colchester
11. Wolves (Graham Turner)
12. Gerry Francis
13. Done Revie, Jock Stein
14. Bobby Charlton, Brian Kidd, Nobby Stiles
15. Saunders, Atkinson, Wylie, Allen
16. Graham Taylor
17. Ferenc Puskas
18. Frank O'Farrell
19. Brian Clough
20. Reading

QUIZ 32

FANATICS & FANZINES

1. Alan Gilzean
2. Don Givens
3. Bournemouth
4. Burnley
5. Watford
6. 36
7. Wycombe Wanderers
8. Literary – Keith Waugh, Alan Dickens, Craig Shakespeare
9. All scored more than 100 goals
10. Frank McLintock
11. Gillingham
12. Reading
13. Birmingham
14. Bradford
15. Man City

ANSWERS

16 Bournemouth

17 Arsenal

18 Hibernian

19 Liverpool

20 Grimsby

21 Aston Villa

22 Sheffield United

23 Newcastle

24 Dartford

25 West Ham

QUIZ 33

THE NAME'S THE SAME

1 Paine

2 Ball

3 Gary Stevens

4 Miller

5 Law (Bonar and Denis)

6 Haynes

7 Lawrence

8 Williams

9 Gilbert

10 Gillespie

11 Channon (Mick and Paul)

12 Kerr (Bobby and Graham)

13 Dickens

14 Daley

15 George

16 Giles

17 Stevenson

18 Brazil

19 Charlton

20 Macdonald

QUIZ 34

EUROPEAN & INTERNATIONAL 2

1 Michel Platini

2 Barcelona (108 170 at the beginning of the 1987–88 season)

3 Malmo, SV Hamburg

4 Brazil

5 Feyenoord

6 Chilean

7 Alessandro Altobelli

8 Alan Mullery

9 Wembley

10 Ray Wilkins (24 – 84 in total)

11 FC Gothenburg

12 Steaua Bucharest

13 Birmingham (25, to Arsenal's 24)

14 Spain (Barcelona, Atletico Madrid and Real Madrid)

15 False – they won in 1968

16 Torino

17 Mexico

18 Ray Houghton

19 West Germany and Italy

20 24

ANSWERS

QUIZ 35

SOCCER & LITERATURE

1   Sir Walter Scott

2   Albert Camus played in goal for Oran

3   William Shakespeare

4   Oscar Wilde

5   Barry Hines

6   Tom Stoppard's

7   David Hay's

8   Barrie Williams

9   *Twelfth Night*

10 *The Good Companions*

11 *They Used to Play on Grass*

12 *Boys From the Black Stuff*

13 Sir Matt Busby

14 Stanley Matthews

15 Derek Hatton

16 Samuel Pepys

17 Arnold Bennett's

18 1930s

19 Kenny Sansom, Bruce Grobbelaar

20 Perryman's autobiography is titled *A Man For All Seasons*, also the title of the play about Thomas More

QUIZ 36

GOALKEEPERS

1   Ray Clemence

2   Pat Jennings

3   Zaire

4   1912

5   Antonio Carbajal

6   Dave Beasant (1988)

7   Ron Springett (France won 5–2)

8   Hans van Breukelen

9   Gordon Banks

10 Martin Taylor, Mark Wallington

11 Frank Swift

12 Felix

13 He saved a penalty

14 Marc de Clerc

15 Gordon West

16 His 41st

17 Harald Schumacher

18 Jan Tomaszewski

19 Lev Yashin

20 North Korea

QUIZ 37

NICKNAMES

1   Norwegian – Erik Thorsvedt

2   Eusebio

3   Aldershot

4   Rotherham (The Merry Millers)

5   Jim Smith

6   Italy

7   Oldham, Wigan

8   Emil Butragueno

9   Notts County, Exeter

10 Crewe, Halifax

11 Tom Finney

12 c)

13 Watford (The Hornets), Brentford (The Bees)

14 Alloa

15 Benfica

16 Vinny Jones of Wimbledon

17 Bernard Lisewski

18 Warboys and Bannister

19 Imre Varadi

20 Grimsby Town's – Harry was their own ubiquitous inflatable

ANSWERS

QUIZ 38

WORLD CUP 2

1 13

2 Four (Uruguay 1930, Italy 1938, Brazil 1958, 1970, England 1966)

3 North Korea

4 Jack Taylor

5 Uruguay

6 Brazil

7 Elkjaer

8 Green

9 Paul Gascoigne

10 Italy (a 1–1 draw in the first game)

11 Ray Wilkins

12 Belgium, France

13 Pele

14 Mario Kempes (1978)

15 200 000 (199 854)

16 Argentina – Holland (1978)

17 15 (drawn nine, lost ten)

18 Hungary

19 Russia (Hungary 6–0), Denmark (Uruguay 6–1)

20 1966

QUIZ 39

GEOGRAPHY TEST 2 – EUROPE

1 G (Bucharest)

2 E (FC Porto)

3 H (Juventus, Turin)

4 I (Nantes)

5 B (Copenhagen)

6 D (Madrid)

7 C (Tirana)

8 A (Napoli)

9 F (Eintracht Frankfurt)

10 J (Prague)

QUIZ 40

BEAT THE INTRO 2

1 Gary Pallister

2 Newcastle United

3 Joe Jordan

4 Real Madrid

5 Tommy Lawton

6 Wolves

7 John Gidman

8 Mansfield Town

9 Don Mackay

10 Leicester City

ANSWERS

QUIZ 41

CRYPTIC CORNER

1 Ajax

2 Jimmy Husband

3 Stamford Bridge

4 Windsor Park

5 Joel Bats

6 Perry Digweed

7 Eric Nixon

8 George

9 Socrates

10 Ernie Moss

11 St Andrews

12 Smith

13 Rothmans

14 Carlton Fairweather

15 Everton (Ever-ton)

16 Sutton United

17 Cologne

18 Tresor

19 Clive Walker

20 Tony Book

QUIZ 42

WHO'S WHO 2

1 Bill Shankly

2 Tony Book

3 Phil Neal

4 Vince Hilaire

5 Mal Donaghy

6 Liam Brady

7 Helmut Schoen

8 Kenny Burns

9 Ted MacDougall

10 Jimmy Adamson

11 Jim Smith

12 Frank Worthington

13 Camacho

14 Roy Wegerle

15 Keith Edwards

16 George Best

17 Tommy Tynan

18 Romeo Zondervan

19 Keith Hackett

20 Bernd Schuster

QUIZ 43

DISCIPLINE & SCANDAL

1 'Mooning'

2 The first player to be shown the red card

3 Paolo Rossi

4 For refusing Cardiff supporters admission

5 The drawn England – Northern Ireland World Cup qualifying game that Romania claimed was fixed

6 Jan Molby

7 Belgium (Ghent)

8 The 1970s (1973)

9 Peter Swan, Tony Kay, David Layne

10 Nine

11 Willie Johnstone

12 Bobby Moore's arrest for the alleged theft of a bracelet

13 Portugal

14 Terry Fenwick

15 Caldere

16 Dusseldorf

17 Fisher Athletic's

18 Internazionale

19 Vinny Jones

20 That it was fixed

ANSWERS

QUIZ 44

FA CUP 2

1   1–0 (33 occasions from 119 matches)

2   John Sissons (18 yr 215 days)

3   The Oval

4   1950s (1955)

5   Arsenal, Liverpool

6   Liverpool 3 Everton 1 (1986)

7   They were relegated from the First Division

8   Tottenham (1982)

9   Houseman, Hutchinson

10   a) Bobby Robson
     b) Ron Greenwood

11   Referee

12   Kevin Moran (1985)

13   Gary Sprake

14   Three – Blackpool 4 Bolton 3

15   Newcastle, Arsenal

16   Coventry – Spurs in 1987

17   1980 – West Ham *v.* Arsenal

18   Eddie Kelly

19   Ian Rush, Bryan Robson, Ricky Villa

20   Aleksic, Stepney, Parkes

QUIZ 45

SCOTTISH FOOTBALL 2

1   Ally McLeod

2   Dumbarton

3   Morton

4   Andy Beattie

5   Andy Gray

6   Martin Buchan

7   John Robertson

8   Partick Thistle

9   The Group of Death

10   Charlie Nicholas

11   Morton

12   Aberdeen

13   1986

14   It was awarded to the entire Scotland World Cup squad

15   Peter Latchford, Johannes Edvaldson

16   Aberdeen, Alloa, Ayr, Arbroath, Albion Rovers, Airdrieonians

17   Roger Hynd

18   *Ally's Tartan Army* by Andy Cameron

19   Paul McStay

20   Stenhousemuir

ANSWERS

QUIZ 46

MIX & MATCH – THE CLASSIFIED

Arsenal	2	Spurs	0	45 129
Coventry	5	Sheffield Wed	0	15 191
Luton	6	Southampton	1	8 637
Middlesbrough	1	Man United	0	24 411
Millwall	1	Charlton	0	17 025
Newcastle	0	Derby	1	30 055
Forest	2	Everton	0	26 008
QPR	1	Norwich	1	12 410
West Ham	1	Wimbledon	2	18 346
Crystal Palace	4	Walsall	0	9 352
Man City	0	Leeds	0	33 034
WBA	4	Shrewsbury	0	18 411
Bristol City	0	Bristol Rovers	1	23 191
Sheffield United	1	Chesterfield	3	15 769
Wolves	3	Chester	1	21 901
Tranmere	2	Burnley	1	7 974

QUIZ 47

NAME THE YEAR

1	1975	18	1984 (Liverpool – Everton)
2	1965	19	1953
3	1985	20	1988
4	1976		
5	1968		
6	1983		
7	1954		
8	1967		
9	1977		
10	1980		
11	1963		
12	1984		
13	1982		
14	1969		
15	1945		
16	1971		
17	1970		

ANSWERS

QUIZ 48

BRITISH FOOTBALL 3

1 Leeds

2 1960s (1962–63)

3 Birmingham

4 True (Arsenal were the first in 1931)

5 Liverpool – Forest (5–0)

6 Nigel Clough

7 Man City, Leeds, Coventry

8 Arsenal

9 Hartlepool

10 Cambridge

11 29

12 Arsenal

13 Because they were relegated to the Third Division

14 St Johnstone

15 Richard Attenborough

16 Football journalists

17 Des O'Connor

18 1949

19 Carlisle

20 5.3

QUIZ 49

THE EIGHTIES

1 Crystal Palace

2 Mark Walters

3 Spurs and Man City

4 Wolves and Burnley

5 The Bradford fire, and the death of a boy following the Birmingham – Leeds game

6 Charlie Nicholas (1987 Littlewoods Cup final)

7 Southend

8 Turkey (October 1987)

9 The Full Members Cup

10 1985–86

11 Colchester

12 1987–88

13 Tommy Hutchison (1981) and Gary Mabbutt (1987)

14 Alessandro Altobelli, 1982

15 Doncaster and Blackburn Rovers

16 The Odsal Stadium

17 1985

18 Dundee United

19 Walsall

20 Canon

QUIZ 50

SOCCER & TV

1 1960s (1964)

2 Arsenal

3 Subbuteo

4 Julie Welch

5 Mike Yarwood

6 Glasgow Rangers

7 Spurs – Forest (1983)

8 Ian St John

9 True (64 countries, 43 of them live)

10 Hazell

11 Norway's

12 1930s (1937)

13 80%

14 Mick Channon's

15 Hull City

16 First game to be transmitted in colour

17 Danny Blanchflower

18 Manchester United

19 Bournemouth

20 *Quizball*

ANSWERS

QUIZ 51

LEFT BACKS

1 Terry Cooper, Paul Madeley, Trevor Cherry

2 Kenny Sansom

3 Nigel Winterburn

4 Mike Pejic

5 Clayton Blackmore

6 Frank Lampard

7 Tony Dorigo

8 Sammy Nelson

9 Duxbury, Gibson, Albiston, Blackmore

10 Briegel

11 Eddie MacReadie

12 Alec Lindsay

13 Mick Mills

14 Ian Dawes

15 Frank Gray

16 Ray Wilson

17 Terry Cooper

18 Pat Van Den Hauwe

19 Bob McNab

20 True

QUIZ 52

EUROPEAN & INTERNATIONAL 3

1 Barcelona

2 True (4)

3 Juventus

4 Venables, Viollet, Viljoen

5 AC Milan

6 Klinsmann

7 Igor Belanov (Dynamo Kiev)

8 Platini, Tigana, Fernandez, Giresse

9 Denmark

10 Graeme Souness (£650 000 to Sampdoria in 1984)

11 Borussia Moenchengladbach, Bayern Munich, FC Cologne, Hamburg

12 Carlos Valderama

13 150

14 Franz Beckenbauer, Karl-Heinz Rummenigge

15 Greece (Athens)

16 Spurs (3)

17 Vancouver, Stings, Cosmos

18 Milan, Rome

19 Nottingham Forest

20 Roma, Sofia, BK 09, Standard

QUIZ 53

PUB GAMES

1 Aston VillA, Charlton AthletiC, LiverpooL, Northampton TowN and York CitY.

2 Springett, Hodgkinson, Banks, Waiters, Bonetti, Stepney, West, Shilton, Clemence, Parkes, Rimmer, Corrigan, Spink, Bailey, Woods and Seaman.

3 Brian Clough, Jimmy Armfield, Jock Stein, Jimmy Adamson, Allan Clarke, Eddie Gray, Billy Bremner and Howard Wilkinson.

4 Sanchez, Whiteside, Hoddle, Brooking, Osborne, Stokes, Porterfield, Clarke, Young and Astle.

5 Blackburn, Blackpool, Bolton, Burnley, Everton, Liverpool, Manchester

ANSWERS

City, Manchester United and Preston.

6   Billy Bremner, Frank McLintock, Gordon Banks, Pat Jennings, Ian Callaghan, Alan Mullery, Kevin Keegan, Emlyn Hughes, Kenny Burns and Kenny Dalglish.

7   Brighton and Hove Albion, Preston North End, Queens Park Rangers, West Bromwich Albion, West Ham United, Heart of Midlothian and Queen of the South.

8   AC Milan, Napoli, Roma, Sampdoria, Internazionale, Juventus, Torino, Fiorentina, Cesena, Verona, Como, Ascoli, Pisa, Pescara, Avellino and Empoli.

9   Joe Jordan, Murdo MacLeod, Arthur Albiston, Gary Gillespie, Robert Russell and Davey Dodds.

10   AlloA, CeltiC, Dundee UniteD, East FifE, East StirlingshirE and KilmarnocK.

11   Aldershot, Arsenal, Barnsley, Blackpool, Bradford, Burnley, Bury, Chelsea, Chesterfield, Darlington, Everton, Fulham, Gillingham, Liverpool, Middlesbrough, Millwall, Portsmouth, Reading, Rochdale, Scarborough, Southampton, Sunderland, Walsall, Watford, Wimbledon and Wrexham.

QUIZ 54

1989

1   Arsenal, Chelsea, Wolves, Wrexham

2   Alan Taylor

3   Sutton United

4   Jock Wallace

5   Ipswich

6   Colin Addison

7   Lee Chapman

8   Because vouchers were available for the impending FA Cup tie with Liverpool

9   Ralph Milne

10   Hartlepool

11   Brian Clough's manhandling of Forest fans who had come on the pitch to celebrate

12   Newcastle

13   Keith Edwards, Tommy Tynan, Ian Rush, John Aldridge and Trevor Francis

14   Dave Bassett

15   Free transfer

16   Yugoslav

17   Ted Croker

18   Gerry Armstrong

19   Greece (1–1)

20   Grimsby (Fifth Round)

ANSWERS

QUIZ 55

TRANSFERS 2

1 Johann Cruyff (Ajax – Barcelona, 1973)

2 Denis Law (Torino – Man United, 1962)

3 David Mills

4 Colchester

5 Paris St Germain

6 Five weeks

7 1977

8 Clive Allen

9 Mirandinha

10 Ron and Peter Springett

11 Laurie Cunningham

12 Cardiff City

13 John Charles (Leeds – Juventus)

14 Andy Walker

15 Ray Houghton

16 Richard Gough

17 Leighton James

18 Stoke City

19 Ascoli

20 Dave Beasant

QUIZ 56

THE BACK PAGE

1 Ossie Ardiles and Ricky Villa

2 Stan Bowles

3 1986 in Mexico, before England World Cup fans arrived

4 1981

5 Gerry Queen, the Crystal Palace striker

6 Robert Maxwell

7 The Heysel tragedy in May 1985

8 Catholics

9 In reference to Maradona's goal invoking 'the hand of God'

10 Racist 'fans'

11 1982

12 The plastic pitch installation at QPR

13 Louis Edwards

14 Lawrie McMenemy and Kevin Keegan

15 1977

16 Manchester United

17 He scored the goal that condemned United to relegation

18 1950

19 The 1986 World Cup

20 Paul Gascoigne

QUIZ 57

THAT'S FOOTBALL, BRIAN

1 The Bundesliga

2 Arsenal

3 Fiat; Agnelli

4 False – 1968

5 Jason Dozell

6 Charlton, Chelsea, Chester, Chesterfield

7 Jackie Milburn

8 Dave Sexton

9 False – Rochdale, 1962

10 QPR

11 First international

12 Wimbledon (7994)

13 Leeds (20 272)

14 Bristol City (9817)

15 Stanley Park

16 Sixth

17 Nine

18 George Courtney

ANSWERS

19   20

20   Argentina

QUIZ 58

92 UP

1   True

2   Michael Thomas

3   Penarol

4   Allan Clarke, Norman Hunter

5   Liverpool

6   Howard Kendall

7   1971

8   Nat Lofthouse

9   11–0

10   Roy McFarland

11   Griffin Park

12   Mark Lawrenson

13   Freight Rover

14   Bath City's

15   European Cup (1961), Fairs Cup (1967)

16   QPR's

17   Alan Biley

18   40 000 (39 900)

19   Peter Beardsley

20   Allan Simonsen

21   Ron Harris

22   Ian Rush

23   True

24   Sixth Round

25   Ian Wallace

26   Aston Villa

27   Jim Cannon

28   David Speedie

29   Frank Stapleton

30   Belle Vue

31   Howard Kendall, Gordon Lee, Harry Catterick

32   Red and white stripes

33   Ray Harford

34   10–0

35   Bill Shankly

36   True

37   Brian Clough

38   Ronnie Radford

39   Mark Lillis

40   Terry Neill

41   Alf Ramsey, Bobby Robson

42   Peter Lorimer

43   1986–87

44   False (1962–63)

45   Graham Taylor

46   Ian Callaghan

47   Steve Foster

48   Rodney Marsh (*Rodney, Rodney*)

49   1967

50   Billy Bingham

51   Colin Todd

52   Barry Kitchener

53   Jackie Milburn

54   Tony Barton

55   Kevin Reeves, Justin Fashanu, Dave Watson

56   True

57   Larry Lloyd

58   Boundary Park

59   Peter Rhoades-Brown

60   Division Three

61   Michael Foot

62   Mark Hateley

63   Beat Spurs in the Third Round

64   Sherpa Van Trophy

65   Runners-up (1976)

66   Simod Cup

67   Spotland

ANSWERS

68 Bobby Mimms

69 Wolves

70 Kevin Keegan

71 Martin Peters

72 Ron Springett

73 Welsh Cup

74 Guernsey

75 Bobby Moore

76 Mike Summerbee

77 One – Stoke are the second oldest

78 Jim Montgomery

79 Two

80 Don Rogers

81 Frank O'Farrell

82 1961

83 The Welsh Cup

84 Alan Buckley

85 False (UEFA Cup 1983–84)

86 Nobby Stiles

87 True

88 Freight Rover

89 Two

90 West Brom

91 Dai Davies

92 Liverpool

ANSWERS

PICTURE QUIZ 1

1 Bryan Robson
2 Gary Lineker
3 Kenny Dalglish
4 Viv Anderson

PICTURE QUIZ 2

1 Sweden
2 Barcelona
3 Michel Platini
4 European Cup Winners Cup

PICTURE QUIZ 3

1 John Shaw
2 Gary Bailey
3 Dave Beasant
4 Pat Bonner

PICTURE QUIZ 4

1 Carlos Valderrama (Colombia)
2 John Barnes
3 Peter Shilton
4 Kevin Keegan

PICTURE QUIZ 5

1 Jan Molby
2 Terry McDermott
3 Denis Law
4 Gary Lineker

PICTURE QUIZ 6

1 Alan Ball
2 St Mirren (in the 1987 Scottish FA Cup final)
3 Kevin Bond
4 Terry Venables

PICTURE QUIZ 7

1 McAvennie, Woods, Butcher and Roberts were charged with a breach of the peace.
2 1880s
3 Ian Bowyer and Brian Flynn
4 Ernie Clay (Fulham)

PICTURE QUIZ 8

1 Ray Wilkins
2 Johnny Byrne
3 Nigel Clough
4 Don Howe

PICTURE QUIZ 9

1 Jesper Olsen
2 Kenny Dalglish
3 Vinny Jones

PICTURE QUIZ 10

1 Brian Kilcline
2 Dale Gordon
3 Charlie Nicholas